EQUAL RITES

EQUAL RITES

*Lesbian and Gay Worship, Ceremonies,
and Celebrations*

Editors
KITTREDGE CHERRY
ZALMON SHERWOOD

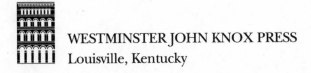

WESTMINSTER JOHN KNOX PRESS
Louisville, Kentucky

Scripture quotations from the Revised Standard Version of the Bible are copyright 1946, 1952, © 1971, 1973 by the Division of Christian Education of the National Council of the Churches of Christ in the U.S.A. and are used by permission.

Book design by Publishers' WorkGroup
Cover design by V. C. Davis

First edition

Published by Westminster John Knox Press
Louisville, Kentucky

This book is printed on acid-free paper that meets the American National Standards Institute Z39.48 standard. ♾

PRINTED IN THE UNITED STATES OF AMERICA

95 96 97 98 99 00 01 02 03 04 — 10 9 8 7 6 5 4 3 2

Library of Congress Cataloging-in-Publication Data

Equal rites : lesbian and gay worship, ceremonies, and celebrations /
  Kittredge Cherry and Zalmon Sherwood, editors. — 1st ed.
       p.   cm.
  Includes bibliographical references.
  ISBN 0-664-25535-3 (alk. paper)
  1. Worship programs.   2. Gays—Religious life.   3. Homosexuality—Religious aspects—Christianity.   I. Cherry, Kittredge, date–.
II. Sherwood, Zalmon O.
  BV199.G39E68   1995
  264'.008'664—dc20   94-3516

Contents

Acknowledgments

As editors of this book, we would like to thank the following individuals:

Chris Glaser, for recommending us to Westminster John Knox Press for this project; Alexa Smith, the Westminster John Knox editor who conceived this book project and obtained her organization's commitment; Stephanie Egnotovich, the Westminster John Knox editor who patiently fielded our questions and skillfully saw our manuscript through publication; Pamela Pasti, our agent, who encouraged us throughout the process; Troy Perry, Nancy Wilson, Ravi Verma, and the entire staff at the Universal Fellowship of Metropolitan Community Churches (UFMCC) International Headquarters, for supporting our efforts; Emily Richards, for assisting Zalmon in Michigan; Audrey E. Lockwood, for her continuing love and devotion to Kittredge during this project and countless others in their nineteen years together; and the many contributors who responded to our invitation to be a part of this anthology. Thanks be to God!

Introduction

Authentic spiritual expression is a basic human need. People long for times and places in which relationships are restored, the meaning of life is regained, and the divine is made real. Worship, a word that means "to make worthy" or "to respect," has the power to affirm our whole selves: body, mind and spirit. Worshiping God, not alone, but in community, generates awareness that all life is sacred and interconnected. The ultimate goal of worship is to empower the community to minister among those in need and to witness on behalf of love and justice.

The time is ripe for a collection of worship services, ceremonies, and celebrations created by lesbian and gay people for use in communities that affirm them. On one hand, the need is overwhelming. Established churches have systematically condemned lesbians and gay men for centuries on moral, biblical, and theological grounds. The result is a tremendous hunger for worship services that honor lesbian and gay experiences. On the other hand, the need is already beginning to be filled. Lesbians and gay men are forming their own faith communities inside and outside the established churches, and ever-increasing numbers of mainline churches are proclaiming that they welcome all people, regardless of sexual orientation. A spiritual renaissance is occurring now among lesbian and gay people of faith around the world.

Who Will Benefit from This Book?

Equal Rites is designed for lesbian and gay people, as well as for anyone seeking to experience the full diversity of God's creation in worship. As co-editors, we approached this book from widely differing backgrounds, which we hope enabled us to present a broad spectrum of material that can be adopted or adapted by many different communities. Our combined experience covers planning and/or participating in worship with congregations that differ in many ways: congregations that are primarily lesbian and gay and those that are primarily heterosexual; congregations in small towns and in huge metropolises throughout the United States and on other continents; gatherings of just a few friends and gatherings of a few thousand; congregations that vary by race, age, and gender; congregations from one denomination and those that are ecumenical or interfaith. We hope that *Equal Rites* will ignite the imagination of people in all these contexts. We endeavored to compile the best liturgies from a wide variety of Christian traditions, while balancing gender and ethnicity. The result draws together the work of some thirty contributors whose backgrounds are described at the end of this volume.

We compiled this collection during a historical period of debate concerning whether there is a place in established churches for lesbian and gay people—and hence, for the services in this book. We acknowledge that lesbians and gay men often have a lot of justifiable anger toward and mistrust of religious institutions. Many of them have been excommunicated because of their homosexuality. Most denominations will baptize but not ordain them, will bury but not marry them. Religious officials have lobbied against equal rights protection in housing and employment, tried to defeat safe-sex education necessary to prevent the spread of AIDS, and contributed to the atmosphere of homophobia that leads to gay bashing and a high suicide rate among lesbian and gay teenagers. The exceptions are too few and far between.

Religious authorities are not the only ones who question whether lesbians and gay men belong in the church. Lesbians and gay men are leaving mainline congregations in legion. They find they can no longer nurture their souls in alienating religious traditions that ignore or deny their existence. Others, raised outside the church, wouldn't dream of entering it, assuming that whatever happens inside is archaic and irrelevant to their own life experience.

We offer this book because we believe that Christianity and the lesbian/gay community have something to offer each other. *Equal Rites* is a collective contribution to the education of mainline congregations as they struggle to be more inclusive of sexual minorities. Lesbians and gay men have been relegated to the margins of traditional Christianity, a difficult position, but also one that affords them insights that can be a blessing for the whole community. Many self-affirming lesbians and gay men have discovered mainline congregations, usually located in urban or academic communities, where the commingling of races and genders, of sexualities and ages, of politics and theologies reflects the comprehensive unity Christians ideally seek. Such inclusivity does not happen overnight but, rather, as a result of sensitive, gifted pastoral leadership and the willingness of participants to stand in the midst of the assembly and be genuine. We also affirm the decision of many lesbians and gay men to form their own faith communities where they experience Christ's love and liberation.

The current blossoming of lesbian/gay spirituality is so enormous that we needed to focus this book in some specific ways. Therefore, *Equal Rites* has a basically Christian framework; we honor the multiple ways that people approach God by incorporating a variety of images. Many of the rites in this book reflect the need to create entirely new types of ceremonies to mark the transition points in lesbian and gay lives. All are written by lesbians or gay men, with the following exceptions: "A Service of Worship for Empowerment," which is a collaborative effort by a group of people with various sexual orientations; the work of Elias Farajaje-Jonez, who identifies as bisexual; and "Eucharistic Prayer for the Powerless, the Oppressed, the Unusual," which though written by a heterosexual woman, came to us from a gay man and impressed us with its beauty.

Although the book includes only rites written in English by lesbians and gay men within the United States, we hope they will prove inspiring to people of faith beyond the borders of our country. Lesbians and gay men are not identical, and we acknowledge the powerful spiritual breakthroughs being made in lesbian-only and gay-only groups. We generally address both groups together in these rites, which celebrate both their common ground and particular differences that enrich the community.

Characteristics of Worship

The technical name for the worship services, ceremonies, and celebrations that take place in the church is *liturgy*. It comes from the Greek words *laos* and *ergos,* which together can be translated simply as "the work of the people." The rituals that take place in the church are a kind of work, the soul's work. Liturgy is a prescribed form of language and ceremony for people to use when they gather with the intention of worshiping in communion and community. The word *liturgy* acts as a reminder that one of humankind's most important works is to praise the Creator together and to dwell with one another in a prayerful manner.

The focus of worship is the Other—the Holy One, the Beyond in Our Midst, the Inexpressible Mystery, God. Here lies the heart of religion, manifested in the awe and care that accompany true spiritual expressions. Liturgy can lift people from the petty confusions of existence and focus their complete attention on the transformations that bind all humankind, indeed all the natural world. Liturgy is communal, not privatized, and it involves a set form, specific procedures, or to use another religious term, ritual.

Ritual is an integral part of life. It provides the actions and forms through which people meet, carry out social activities, celebrate, and commemorate. Whether the acts appear casual or dramatic, sacred or secular, they express a meaning and significance that extend beyond the particular event itself. Rituals, like myths, address the urge to comprehend human existence; the search for a marked pathway as one moves from one stage of life to the next; the need to establish secure and fulfilling relationships within the human community; and the longing to know one's part in the vast wonder and mystery of the cosmos.

Worship awakens awareness of both unity and diversity. Whenever and wherever people truly worship, they need to understand that they are not isolated individuals or communities, but a part of a global family. A good litmus test for worship is its ability to spark forward movement in a community. Worship expresses what a community believes, what it has experienced, and what it hopes for. True worship honors the many distinctions within and beyond the worshiping community, such as race, culture, gender, class, age, physical ability, or sexual orientation.

Worship needs a definite rhythm, a way to achieve for the community at least a fragment of continuity, regularity, predictability, coherence. Worship is an art, not a science. To practice such an art requires shouldering the responsibility and discipline of creating a beautiful event. Worship as art helps people breathe in beauty and make it part of themselves. Artistic expression in worship can also create a context in which the horrors of the world's injustice and brokenness can be redeemed. Music, dance, poetry, drama, and the visual arts can be used in effective ways during worship as an offering of the creative gifts of the worshiping community.

Language is always influential and formative, but it may have special impact in times of worship because, ideally, the congregation is using all five of the senses to make contact with the divine. Inclusive language has developed to reflect the fullness of God and creation. The best-known aspect of inclusive language is the elimination of sexist language; for example, humanity is not referred to in exclusively male or female terms, and God is described as either genderless or both masculine and feminine. Inclusive language jars some people at first, but later these same people often report that it has opened the way for them to experience new dimensions of the divine. The growing use of inclusive language in worship reflects a serious commitment to use words more responsibly, to speak more precisely, and to communicate sensitively.

Imagery and symbols are closely related to language. During worship, symbols not only instruct people, but also move them and open up levels of reality that otherwise would remain closed. Things that are common and natural—water, light, fire, darkness, earth, bread, wine—make effective symbols. The most potent symbols have multiple meanings, yet do not need lengthy explanation. Symbols derive their power from the fact that they reflect parts within each person. Symbols chosen for use in worship have personal significance and translate into a more communal, universal dimension of shared experience.

Where there is authentic ritual, there is always full participation according to each person's capabilities and desires. The emphasis in worship should be on how all participants can give and receive fully, using their whole bodies and all their senses: sight, smell, taste, hearing, touch. At its roots, Christianity is a very physical, embodied faith. Its central ritual, the Eucharist, consists of eating and drinking "the body and blood of Christ."

The body has been effectively banished from most mainline worship. Movement is inhibited by stationary pews and worship books. Other Christian traditions encourage clapping, dancing, kneeling, and other physical expressions of worship. Religious leaders have much to learn from gay men and lesbians, for when they come out and affirm themselves in the face of social oppression, they affirm the basic goodness of human sexuality and embodiment.

Characteristics of Worship That Affirm
Lesbians and Gay Men

Lesbians and gay men are starved for words of life, for symbolic forms that wholeheartedly affirm their personhood. The belief that lesbian and gay experiences are valid and worthy of reflection is the foundation of worship that affirms lesbians and gay men. The call for new rites by lesbians and gay men assumes that existing liturgies do not have a monopoly on the words of truth or the power of salvation. Traditional worship's message for sexual minorities is so ambivalent, irrational, and nonsensical, its power so negative, that attendance at such rites can poison lesbian/gay souls. Worship has become all too often an occasion of sin rather than redemption, a place from which lesbians and gay men come away angry and frustrated rather than enlightened and healed.

Each generation and nation needs to hear and speak the gospel in its own tongue. The word translated as "nation" in many Bible passages is the Greek word *ethnos,* which refers to a race, culture, or people. The lesbian/gay community shares a common culture and has its own history, vocabulary, symbols, institutions, and values. Today's "Queer Nation" needs to hear the gospel in its own idiom.

Specific linguistic issues arise when worship grows out of lesbian and gay experiences. Some lesbian and gay people are particularly sensitive to the need for inclusive language because of their position on the border between gender roles. Although "lesbian" and "gay" are commonly accepted as the most generic terms, a growing number prefer to call themselves "queer," thereby redeeming an old slur and adopting one word to encompass not only lesbians and gay men, but also bisexuals, transsexuals, and all sexual outcasts. Other epithets are also being reclaimed by people who proudly proclaim themselves as "dykes," "fags," and the like. Sensitivity is also needed to refer appropriately to heterosexual supporters of lesbian/gay rights; they may be "our families and friends," "affirming," "supporters," "allies," "those who stand with us," or perhaps just "queer" too.

Lesbians and gay men are in need of a greater ability, perhaps even a greater willingness, to live symbolically. They make the best they can of their circumstances without, for the most part, the benefit of inspiring myths and rituals that are attuned to the unique needs of sexual minorities. All lesbians and gay men have suffered the loss of positive self-images as a direct result of their second-class status and consequent objectification in a heterosexual-dominant society. It is painful to consider the countless lives wasted, the talents atrophied, and the sickness suffered by sexual minorities who were never allowed, much less encouraged, to know themselves and take strength and happiness in that knowledge. Rites play an important role in offering lesbians and gay men images and symbols that affirm their experience.

Lesbian/gay-positive worship should combine more universal symbols, like flowers and shells, with specific symbols from gay and lesbian experience. Symbols in worship might include art and photographs that address the lesbian/gay experience; icons or pictures of historical and contemporary prophets who have struggled for lesbian/gay rights; lavender, a combination of pink and blue traditionally associated with female and male; and the rainbow, representing diversity and transformation.

Other international symbols relevant to lesbian/gay experience include two female or two male signs linked; the pink triangle, which was worn by gay prisoners in Nazi concentration camps; and the Greek letter *lambda,* which represents synergy and serves as a symbol of lesbian/gay liberation.

Much symbolism stems from the Stonewall Rebellion, whose anniversary is commemorated by most lesbian/gay pride festivals. On June 29, 1969, sexual minorities at New York City's Stonewall Inn fought back against police harassment, an action often considered the start of the modern lesbian/gay rights movement. In some contexts, it might be appropriate to use symbols specific to one aspect of lesbian and gay life: the red ribbon, worn on the lapel to show solidarity with and compassion for those living with AIDS; the Names Project Quilt, a patchwork memorial to those who have died from AIDS; or a labrys, a double-headed ax that has become a lesbian symbol.

Lesbians and gay men, deprived of official ceremonies for intimate bonding, often use the term "lover" to describe their life partners. As a result, God as Lover is a potent image, connoting those who have the courage to touch and make life holy. Some people go a step farther and refer to "Great Gay Spirit" or "Lesbian God"; the freedom to envision a God who shares a same-sex orientation can help heal internalized homophobia.

Images that focus on God's presence with humanity, and even on God's vulnerability, may be especially appropriate for lesbian/gay-oriented worship. Power images such as Judge and Father that emphasize divine omnipotence can be problematic because they have been used to oppress lesbian and gay people. Depending on the worship context, lesbians, gay men, and their supporters may respond well to such images as Gentle One, Justice Seeker, Giver of Hope, Compassionate One, Healer, Comforter, Companion, Creator, Lover, Amazing Grace, Liberator, Risk Taker, and Friend of the Poor. What is important is that each image used in worship contribute to the contemplation of liberation and help set the agenda for the work and play of a free community of gay men, lesbians, and their allies.

Many lesbian and gay people are suspicious of the Bible because it has been used to condemn them. Although the Bible was written in a patriarchal, heterosexist culture, the story of God's love for all people still shines through. Cutting-edge biblical scholars are reclaiming passages that affirm lesbian and gay people, such as the love between Ruth and Naomi, Jonathan and David, Jesus and Lazarus, and Jesus and the beloved disciple. A pertinent subject of recent inquiry concerns "eunuchs." The Hebrew and Greek terms seem to have much broader meaning than is commonly associated with eunuchs today and may have referred to anyone who did not procreate. Understanding the original meaning gives new life to passages such as God's promise, "To the eunuchs who keep my sabbaths, who choose the things that please me and hold fast my covenant, I will give, in my house and within my walls, a monument and a name better than sons and daughters" (Isa. 56:4–5).

In addition to the sacred scriptures of religious traditions, a great variety of other readings are appropriate for lesbian/gay worship. Poetry, musical compositions, dramatic readings, and brief excerpts from the writings by or about lesbian/gay saints, martyrs, prophets, heroines, and heroes can all be mined for their pertinence to the occasion of worship. The pantheon of lesbian/gay writers, artists, musicians, actors, athletes, politicians, scholars, and religious leaders provides a vast legacy from which to craft worship.

Much groundwork in creating lesbian/gay worship has been done by the Universal Fellowship of Metropolitan Community Churches (UFMCC), which has established nearly three hundred congregations throughout the United States and in sixteen other countries. Since its founding in 1968, UFMCC has opened its doors to thousands of lesbians, gay men, and their families and friends, providing an invaluable ministry of healing, community building, and social action. In addition, virtually every mainline denomination has a lesbian/gay caucus, ranging from Dignity (Roman Catholic), Integrity (Episcopal), and Axios (Orthodox) to American Baptists Concerned and Affirmation (United Methodists). (A complete listing of national lesbian/gay caucuses, with contact information, appears in the Appendix.) Many denominations also have networks of congregations that have declared their openness to lesbian and gay people, such as the More Light Congregations of the Presbyterian Church.

Creative, inspiring, meaningful worship is taking place within UFMCC, denominational lesbian/gay caucuses, and affirming congregations. Such organizations offer a starting point for exploring models of liberating worship for sexual minorities. They offer a rich storehouse of talent and materials that contribute greatly to the spiritual formation of lesbians and gay men.

How to Use This Book

Equal Rites is a reference book for creating worship services, ceremonies, and celebrations that are attuned to the unique needs of sexual minorities. Crafting worship involves articulating the aspirations of the community assembled for celebration. Merely to transplant heterosexual and hetero-sexist models of worship will not work. Worship that is done with real intention and meaning requires a lot of energy.

When planning liturgy, people may want to seek advice from supportive religious leaders who have the skills to suggest forms and materials appro-priate for worship. Clergy, musicians, artists, and educators can all make valuable suggestions for effective worship practices, which must then be selected and adapted for the particular context. It may take considerable time to prepare and also to assimilate it afterward, or it may seem to spring almost spontaneously when a few are gathered in God's name. Worship is most effective when done with simplicity, grace, and humility, a moving event during which there are no star performers but rather a series of sacred moments shared by the community.

As editors, we are aware of how an overreliance on written liturgy can rob worship of one of its most crucial elements: spontaneity. During worship, the congregation needs to pray not out of books, but out of the depths of their hearts. However, *Equal Rites* stands as a testament to our belief in the value of writing down the format and text for worship. Written liturgy does more than serve the local community in which it is used; it provides a record so that the spiritual insights of a particular community can be shared with people in other parts of the world and with future generations. Lesbians and gay men, so often erased from official histories, commit a radical act of faith by recording their worship life. The rites presented here are just a fraction of the increasing body of worship material available. May *Equal Rites* contribute to the compendium of ideas and resources from which lesbians and gay men can create their own works of worship.

The rites in this book are not intended to be performed verbatim by various faith communities. Rather, the contributors offer them as models, examples, outlines for occasions of worship that address significant aspects of lesbian/gay spirituality. Virtually all the contributors recommended inclusifying the biblical texts that are used. As contributor Christine Nusse wrote when she submitted her work, "To prepare a liturgy is like preparing a meal. This analogy is very rich and brings out a lot of similarities. For instance, the same liturgy will never be celebrated exactly the same way, just as a recipe will not taste the same twice. Both need a few basic guidelines, a script if you wish, upon which the participants will weave their own gifts, spontaneous or prepared.''

Whatever else moves people to worship, they gather because of a sense, however hidden, that time and place and life need to be sanctified and recreated. The search for holy times and places is itself an expression of human hunger for the transformation of everyday existence. Authentic worship will allow lesbians and gay men to find their voices and express them. It will enable them to find ears that listen to the impassioned voices that suffering creates. Worship awakens awe and reverence among people, allowing them to adopt visions of peace and justice.

Equal Rites begins with a series of rituals that make the connections between baptism and coming out of the closet to acknowledge a lesbian or gay sexual orientation. We believe that coming out is the most powerful, liberating act of worship for lesbians and gay men. It marks the washing away of an old, false self and the birth of a life-giving new identity in community. Coming out begins the journey of exodus from heterosexism to liberation. By making their love visible, lesbians and gay men assert that they will put their bodies on the line to live authentically as God created them to live.

Several contributors to *Equal Rites* told us that this book carries their dreams—dreams for the future when the church will truly welcome lesbians and gay men, their families and friends; dreams for the day when, as Gregory Flaherty wrote in the cover letter for his liturgies, ''we will ourselves become bread and wine, oil and water, word and action, speaking to our world of the time of bent plowshares and peaceful lions.'' Worship that liberates is powerful because it gathers the tears of the past and the dreams of the future into the hearts of those desiring to live fully in the present.

1

Rites to Mark
Spiritual Beginnings

Rites of passage help people traverse those crucial moments when they pass from one state of being to the next, such as birth, adolescence, graduation, romance, commitment, anniversary, retirement, and death. Perhaps the most significant of passages for lesbians and gay men is that of coming out of the closet to acknowledge their sexual orientation. A public ritual for coming out symbolizes an individual's awareness as a sexual minority.

Coming out is a kind of letting go, a difficult process of anger and mourning over estranged familial relationships and lost professional possibilities, a process of grieving for what life "might have been" otherwise. While confronting the pain and losses of coming out, liturgies can do much to celebrate the new life and self-knowledge, the honesty and integrity of the person coming out.

Connections can be made between coming out and baptism, the traditional initiation process during which a Christian community welcomes new members. The use of water in baptism symbolizes washing away a person's sinful nature and marks a person's rebirth to a new life in Christ. For lesbians and gay men of faith, both coming out and baptism are ways to celebrate spiritual beginnings.

COMING OUT: COMING HOME

Diann L. Neu

A rite of coming out needs to be celebrated in every corner and city center of the world, for lesbian women and gay men live everywhere.

Coming out is both a one-time event and a lifetime process. Once someone says out loud to herself or to someone else that she is lesbian, she is always choosing to tell her story again and again and again. Living as an openly lesbian or gay person in this historical time means going against heterosexual norms and often encountering people who just don't understand. Yet, ironically, coming out and living out mean coming home. It says, "I am who I am."

This ritual celebrates coming out and being out. It is written for a lesbian coming-out, but can easily be changed for a gay male coming-out or a joint lesbian and gay coming-out. Use it as a model for the one you or friends need to celebrate.

Preparation

Buy a lavender candle, chimes, water pitcher, and basket that will be given as gifts to the person coming out. Gather a bowl for the water, an evergreen branch to sprinkle water, a loaf of bread, a glass of wine, and a glass of juice. Place these on a central altar table that is covered with a special cloth.

Naming the Circle

ONE: We are here to celebrate N.'s coming out and living out. Congratulations, N., for knowing yourself and for telling others who you are.

Let's create our circle of support by each in turn speaking our names, acknowledging our support of N., and giving a hand to the person next to us as a sign of support. (*Sharing.*)

N., feel the love and support of this circle of friends and family. (*Raise the joined hands.*) Remember it when times are tough, and they will be some days. We love you. And collectively sing that it is good for the world when we come out.

Song

"Good for the World"
Holly Near, adapted by Diann L. Neu

Good for the world for coming out
(*Repeat line three times.*)
When we come out, it's good for the world.

Good for the world for opening doors
(*Repeat line three times.*)
When we open doors, it's good for the world.

Good for the world for telling the truth
(*Repeat line three times.*)
When we tell the truth, it's good for the world.

Good for the world for sharing support
(*Repeat line three times.*)
When we share support, it's good for the world.

Blessing of the Four Elements

ONE: Let us bless the elements of the universe—fire, air, water, and earth—for they have called home to the world our friend, N. (*Four blessers, in turn, bless four elements.*)

BLESSER OF FIRE: South

(*The blesser walks to the center-south and lights a candle on the altar.*)

> Source of Fire,
> O Searing Flame,
> Fill N.'s heart and all our hearts with a spark of passion.
> Empower us and every lesbian and gay person with courage to
>   emerge from cocoons of hibernation and isolation.
> Release our imaginations from their hiding places.
> Guiding Light,
> Fire of Justice,
> One Who Brings Us Home,
> Amen. Blessed be. Let it be so.

BLESSER OF THE AIR: East

(*The blesser walks to the center-east and plays the chimes on the altar.*)

> Source of Air,
> O Whispering Wind,
> Fill N.'s lungs and all our lungs with the breath of healing.
> Blow away the staleness.

Bring freshness into our lives.
Gentle Breeze,
Rustling Sound,
One Who Brings Us Home.
Amen. Blessed be. Let it be so.

BLESSER OF WATER: West
(*The blesser walks to the center-west, pours water into the bowl, dips the evergreen branch, and sprinkles participants with water from the branch.*)
Source of Water,
Ever-bubbling Spring,
Fill N.'s being and all our beings with emotions that flow freely.
Wash away the hurts and pains of all oppressed people.
Quench our thirst for spiritual and sexual connection.
Ocean Womb,
Wellspring of Life,
One Who Brings Us Home.
Amen. Blessed be. Let it be so.

BLESSER OF EARTH: North
(*The blesser walks to the center-north and places a basket of bread on the altar.*)
Source of Earth,
Mother of Our Being,
Fill N.'s body and all our bodies with courage for loving one
    another.
Cradle and protect us as we discover our real selves.
Enlighten us with dreams, visions, and inner wisdom.
Sacred Ground,
Fertile Soil,
One Who Brings Us Home.
Amen. Blessed be. Let it be so.

Chant

"The Earth, the Air, the Fire, the Water"
Source unknown, recorded on Libana *A Circle Is Cast*, ca. 1986.

Reading

"Invisible for Too Long"
LEADER: For a very long time I have wanted to reach out to you in
    solidarity, to work with you to transform injustice . . .
        . . . but I've been invisible for too long.

ALL: Come out, come out, wherever you are!

LEADER: I work next to you in so many places. I'm the doctor who comforted your dying mother. I'm the teacher of your nine-year-old daughter. I'm the therapist who helped you free yourself . . .

. . . but I've been invisible for too long.

ALL: Come out, come out, wherever you are!

LEADER: I stand beside you in so many places. I'm the minister who marched next to you as we advocated for a woman's right to choose. I'm the nun who works at the women's shelter where you volunteer. I'm the social worker at the mental health center who works with your sister . . .

. . . but I've been invisible for too long.

ALL: Come out, come out, wherever you are!

LEADER: I'm your invisible sister, your invisible brother. I've been invisible for too long. I yearn to be known for who I am. As you come out, you give me courage . . .

. . . I yearn to be visible.

ALL: Come out, come out, wherever you are!

Telling the Story of Coming Out

ONE: N., you have listened to this call. You have chosen to be visible. Tell us your story of coming out.

(*The person who is coming out and living out shares her story with the participants.*)

Honoring the Person

LEADER: Thank you, N., for trusting us enough to share your journey with us. We respect you. We honor you. We support and affirm you.

(*Participants respond by sharing words of support and affirmation.*)

LEADER: And we would like to honor you with a few mementos.

N., this candle (*lifts the candle from the altar*) symbolizes your passion for truth. When you burn it, and every candle, reignite this spark. (*Give her the candle.*)

N., these chimes (*play them*) symbolize the unique melody that is yours. When you play them, remember your powerful story. (*Give her the chimes.*)

N., this water pitcher (*hold the pitcher that is on the altar*) symbolizes the deep well that you are. When you pour water from it, hear your pains and hurts splash away. (*Give her the water pitcher.*)

N., this basket of bread (*hold the basket from the altar*) symbolizes the nourishment that you are to us and to others you meet. When you use this basket, visualize the many ways you fill others with your gifts. (*Give her the basket.*)

(*Other words are spoken and gifts are given.*)

Litany of Thanksgiving

LEADER: Gracious God and Loving Goddess, we praise you for creating N. a lesbian. We praise you for creating us, your lesbian, gay, bisexual, transgendered, and heterosexual people.

LEADER: For bringing us out of our closets and into full life,

ALL: We praise you.

LEADER: For embracing us with your love and care,

ALL: We praise you.

LEADER: For giving us a company of friends and a family of choice,

ALL: We praise you.

LEADER: For teaching us that our sexuality is a gift for the community,

ALL: We praise you.

LEADER: For strengthening us to cope with misunderstanding, fear, and hatred,

ALL: We praise you.

LEADER: For helping us break through the heterosexism and homophobia in ourselves, our families and friends, our culture and society, our churches and synagogues,

ALL: We praise you.

LEADER: For enlightening us with dreams of holy impatience,

ALL: We praise you.

(*Add additional lines of praise.*)

LEADER: Gracious God and Loving Goddess, we praise you for creating N. a lesbian. We praise you for creating us, your people.

Blessing of Bread

(*The person who has come out holds the bread and prays:*)

ONE: Blessed are you, Holy Lover, for nourishing us and bringing us home.

Blessing of the Fruit of the Vine

(*A close friend holds glasses of wine and juice and prays:*)

FRIEND: Blessed are you, Gracious Source, for quenching our thirst and bringing us home.

Blessing of the Festive Meal

(*Another friend extends her hands over the food and prays:*)
FRIEND: Blessed are you, Nourishing Mother, for giving us friends to feed our hunger and bring us home.

Song

"We're Coming Home" by Carolyn McDade, © 1991
(*Carolyn McDade's tapes and books can be obtained from Carolyn McDade, P.O. Box 510, Wellfleet, Massachusetts 02667.*)

Greeting of Peace

LEADER: Today N. has come out and come home. We have each come home. Filled with the spirit of this resting place, let us embrace one another in love.
(*Greeting.*)

Sharing a Festive Meal

LEADER: Let us share our festive meal.

A COMING-OUT LITURGY

Malcolm Boyd

(*A participant who is coming out stands in the midst of a community of supportive persons, and before a leader. Everyone present forms a circle.*)

LEADER: Have you decided that you want to come out?
PARTICIPANT: I have.
LEADER: What do you want to come out of?
PARTICIPANT: Repression.
LEADER: What kind of repression?
PARTICIPANT: I am *a gay man/a lesbian.* I have suffered the repression of not feeling that I could share my true identity with other people.
COMMUNITY: We welcome you.
LEADER: Have you felt isolation and loneliness?
PARTICIPANT: I have. The cold waters of fear have covered my body and wounded my soul. I have sensed desolation and utter aloneness. I

have suffered misunderstanding and have even been greeted by others as someone who was a total stranger to me.

LEADER: Have you felt condemnation and rejection?

PARTICIPANT: I have. It seemed sometimes that I was in a prison where I was cruelly mistreated. I was granted no dignity, human warmth, or tenderness. Instead I was treated as a stereotype, not a person. The world condemned me as an outcast, while the church condemned me as a sinner. I felt absolutely rejected on the basis of who I am as created by God in God's image.

COMMUNITY: We offer you affirmation and acceptance as you are.

LEADER: Have you suffered personal attack and spiritual injury?

PARTICIPANT: I have. Angry voices have been raised against me when I tried to be myself and tell the truth about myself. When I saw and heard how other gay people were treated, I felt that I would never be able to come out myself. Listening to the hatred in anti-gay statements felt like a terrible attack on me personally. It has been a deep spiritual injury to live in fear, suffer disastrous wounds to my self-esteem, hear other gays maligned, and realize I was loathed, whether I ever came out of the closet or not.

COMMUNITY: We offer you healing and spiritual sustenance.

LEADER: Have you been forced to play a dishonest role in order to survive?

PARTICIPANT: I have. My family seemed often to require it, at least to desire it. At school it was necessary, and whenever I dropped my mask I was punished. The same was true of my life at work where I sought acceptance and advancement. What I had to confront made me feel confused, emotionally fatigued, and often worthless. Any kind of a relationship posed a threat and a danger. I wondered how much rejection I could stand. When I reached out for understanding or help, I usually received yet another rebuke. However, I just could not be who I'm not. It nearly killed me when I tried so hard and found it hopeless.

COMMUNITY: We offer you validation for yourself as you have been created and celebration of your gayness as a gift of God.

LEADER: What do you seek now to do with your life?

PARTICIPANT: I seek freedom. I want to be myself and find acceptance and love. I never want to have to wear a mask again. I want other people to appreciate me for who I really am. I want to make an honest contribution to life in an open way, without any lies or ambiguity.

COMMUNITY: We offer you the assurance of freedom.

LEADER: What else can we offer you that you feel you need?

PARTICIPANT: I want you to embrace my body and nurture my soul.
(*Each member of the community exchanges the Kiss of Peace with him or her, and with each other, with warm hugs and kisses and spiritual fervor.*)
PARTICIPANT: I thank you for your gift of hospitality. I am ready now to set my feet on the path to freedom. I realize there are other, and perhaps deeper, closets within my life. I wish to come out of these, too, and ask your nurturing guidance to help me. I see that all of life needs to be a coming-out process of growth and ever-new openness. I want to participate in it and be a part of it.
LEADER: You have chosen the path of liberation, of openness, of growth in the spirit and love of God.
COMMUNITY: We offer you our continuing hospitality and support. There are no barriers between us. We are all, always, coming out together in wonderful new ways in the grace of God. We love you.

COMING-OUT RITE:
I ACKNOWLEDGE MY QUEER IDENTITY

Zalmon Sherwood

This rite takes place outdoors, in a field, in a woods, on a beach during the night. Participants gather around a fire. Music by guitar, flute, drums, or other portable instruments would be appropriate.

Opening Music

Opening Words

ALL: God is present among us,
in our bodies breathing together, in our hearts beating,
in our music playing, in our fire burning,
in the water flowing, in the stars at midnight,
in our brother's courage, in our lives embracing.
God is present among us.
READER: Courageous One, you have loved us since you breathed life into us. Hear our voices this day as we cry unto you. As members of a sexual minority, we are denied the very life you gave us.
ALL: We hunger, we thirst, we struggle for life.
Hear our cry unto you: for here on earth, we are not heard.
You created us in your image, but we are treated as less than the dust from which we are made.
You call us to serve, but our service is rejected and denied.

Bless us, Liberator of our Souls;
let us not become hardened, let us not become cold,
let us not become bitter or cynical.
Keep our hearts soft and pliant, able to nurture and love with
    compassion and hope.
Keep us in your image that we may be lifegivers
even in the midst of death;
that we may be lovers where there is no love;
that we may be creators of new dreams
where there is no vision.
All this we ask that your spirit might fill us
and your love be made known through us.

READER: We lesbians and gay men are rejected because people are so quick to believe false images, or so bound to see what they want to see that they can't face the truths in front of their eyes.

ALL: You shall know the truth, and the truth shall set you free.

READER: We look around at your beautiful creation, so filled with diversity and complexity. Yet everything has a place and a purpose.

ALL: You shall know the truth, and the truth shall set you free.

READER: We ourselves, each one of us, in our uniqueness, are part of a whole, a part to be valued, accepted, and affirmed.

ALL: You shall know the truth, and the truth shall set you free.

READER: Holy Truth, teach us to see the goodness of ourselves. Erase all prejudice, granting wisdom to those who are afraid. Give the human family open minds, open hearts, eyes of wonder, and a will attuned to justice.

ALL: You shall know the truth, and the truth shall set you free.

ONE COMING OUT: In coming out as a gay man, I am learning to trust my own voice, to follow the lead of my own heart.

    Tonight is just the beginning as I acknowledge my queer identity among you, my friends, whose support and love and encouragement and presence mean so much to me.
    Coming out has been a painful process for me.
    I think of those people who are not here tonight—
    my parents, my siblings, my coworkers, who, for various reasons, cannot bear the thought of my loving another man.
    I miss them, the ones who aren't here, and I hope before long they will speak to me again. May their hatred and fear decrease as more of us proclaim the love we cannot hide.

ALL: Weaver of Souls, out of the expanding energy of creation you have spun each of us into a unique, colorful strand with our own special hue and texture.

You have woven us together into a single family that blankets the globe.

We admit that we have rent the fabric of your design.

We have allowed ourselves to be bound by the narrow contexts of race, age, sex, and ideology.

Open our hearts that we may once again celebrate the wonder of the human fabric and dignity of all.

Reading

Read a selection from Walt Whitman's *Leaves of Grass* (or use some other reading selected by the person coming out).

Period of Silence

Personal Reflections

(*Participants may offer personal reflections on the reading, and on its significance to the person coming out, or share personal anecdotes about the person's growth and development as a human being.*)

Musical Offering

ONE COMING OUT: My friends, it is without fear or shame that I stand with you, declaring my solidarity as a gay man with you and proclaiming my love for you. I open my hands to you as a symbol of what I have to offer you—openness, honesty, freedom, acceptance, and respect—gifts you have offered me, ever so patiently, during the past turbulent months of struggling with my sexual identity. I hope you will continue to assist me during the rough passages I will encounter while coming out. But tonight, and forever, I hope you will rejoice in this miraculous transformation that has taken place in my life: my discovery that the only life worth living is that of a gay man completely out of the closet.

ALL: To be out is divine, to trust and not be afraid.

Coming out is strength and a song to the world.

We sing to you, dear friend, courageous one.

Tonight, you light the spark, you fan the fire,

you steep our sense in desire that all lesbians and gay men

might come out with open hearts.

Your act tonight is of the deepest importance to us.

We commit ourselves to moving forward with you.
(*A period of singing, drumming, dancing, and refreshment follows this rite.*)

RITE OF WELCOME

D. B. Gregory Flaherty

This rite is designed to welcome one who has come to a realization of the gift of homosexuality. It is meant to take place within the lesbian and gay community as a celebration for friends and family as well as the community itself.

Opening Prayer

LEADER: Creating God, you fill the earth with your splendor and our lives with your wonder. You create us in such diversity of skin and limb, eyes and hands, ideas and insights. You fill us with love that draws us closer to each other and to you.

As this day draws to a close, we celebrate the gift of our sister N. and the awareness you bring us through our interaction with each other. May N. see in this vigil of light our support and love for her and your delight in her journey and dance. We ask this through Christ our Light.

ALL: Amen.

Psalm

Psalms suggested for this rite include Ps. 114:1–8, Ps. 118:19–29, Ps. 139:1–18, Ps. 141:6, 8–9, and Ps. 145:1–11.

Scripture

(*Scripture should be selected by the person being celebrated.*)

Reflection

(*This reflection should address the brokenness and healing associated with the coming-out process, as well as offer the community's pledge of support.*)

Blessing

(*After the reflection, the person being celebrated comes forward to a large bowl of water. The person's sponsor stands behind her with her hand on her shoulder. The community is asked to pray a blessing over the water and the person being celebrated. The person then places her hand into the water and generously blesses herself with water in the sign of the cross to symbolize both the pain and the new life that derive from the realization of one's sexuality.*)

ONE BEING CELEBRATED: I was called by name at baptism into the bath of death to new life. I stepped into pain and suffering so as to come out into a new way of living. I now realize that I regard myself as a member of the homosexual community. Aware of the pain this will bring, I also am witness to the new life it carries. Will you support me in my journey, just as you have received life-giving acceptance from each other?

ALL: Yes, N., we do support and welcome you.

Sign of Peace

(*Members of the community may greet and embrace the person being celebrated and one another.*)

Closing Prayer

ONE: God of Light, you shine through our lives in the eyes and voices of each other. Bless our night with your radiance.

ALL: Bless us, God.

ONE: Mother of Creation, you fashion us and gift us with an array of creativity and growth. Bless our days with your color.

ALL: Bless us, God.

ONE: Father of Mercy, you keep us in your care through our support and service to each other. Bless N. and our community with continued acceptance and openness.

ALL: Bless us, God.

ONE: May God truly bless us then, Creator, Redeemer, and Sanctifier.

ALL: Amen.

CHRISTIAN BAPTISMAL COVENANT LITURGY: A CELEBRATION OF THE FEMININE DIVINE

Stephen J. Moore

First Reading: Mark 1:9–10

Second Reading: Galatians 3:26–27

Call of Covenant

ONE: As followers of the historical Jesus of Nazareth, we gather this day to celebrate the wonder of who we are—a gathering of loving, spiritual people. Today we gather with friends and loved ones to celebrate this particular moment in our spiritual journeys together, a moment of dedication to God's dominion of steadfast love. Today we celebrate a new covenant of baptism, a liturgical celebration of our Mother God's unconditional love for all her children, for all of creation. As part of creation, we enter baptism as co-creators of our Mother God's dominion, bringing new birth to our community and our universe by sowing the seeds of love and justice in our world. This new sowing of love embraces the gifts of human wisdom, sexuality, compassion, joy, and the praxis of justice. Today we celebrate the embodiment of these gifts in humanity through the persons who present themselves today for a new covenant of baptism. For as they share their gifts of ministry with us, the co-creation of God's dominion becomes freshly alive in our community and in our world.

Invocation

ONE: Loving and gracious Spirit, we invoke your many names to be with us in this present moment. We rejoice in the blessings of each person here who has come to celebrate with you a new covenant of baptism. For humanity is part of your creative energy in the world. Send us your Holy Spirit, the breath of life. May she fill our gathering with many gifts as we embrace your nurturing love for us. In your many names, we pray. Amen.

Blessing of the Water

(*The baptismal covenant can be used in many different liturgical styles. Through the centuries baptism has existed in many diverse forms in Christian practice. These include but are not limited to sprinkling, pouring, and immersion techniques. The liturgy used here practices a somewhat different technique. Baptismal water is poured over the hands of the baptismal officiant(s) into a baptismal font. These hands, filled with water from the pouring, are then placed on the forehead of the individual person(s) being baptized. This pouring and hand placement occurs in the liturgy at the section called "Rite of Baptism.")*

ONE: The creator God was busy giving birth over her creation, groaning in the labor pains of love to bring forth the gifts of our universe into existence. And the Spirit of God, the breath of life, hovered over the crystal green and blue waters of the earth.

MANY: She hovered over creation, bringing forth the *dabhar,* the word, the creative energy of God.

ONE: And from the waters of creation came forth the gracious blessings of all life. And all that lived drew its strength and nourishment. The *dabhar* was spoken. All living things came into being.

MANY: She brought forth humanity as well, fashioned in her own image, female and male she created them.

ONE: And she blessed them with the gifts of diverse sexuality, creativity, and compassion. For the breath of life, God's Spirit, breathed life into humanity and all living things. And through the waters of the womb and the waters of creation, life sprang forth in abundance and diversity.

MANY: When the time was ripe, God's Spirit gathered together the children of Israel as a spiritual community and called them out of their oppression and bondage into the blessings of freedom.

ONE: God's Spirit led them through the waters of the Jordan River into a promised land.

MANY: And when the time was ripe, God's Spirit brought forth Jesus of Nazareth, protected and nurtured in the compassionate waters of his mother's womb.

ONE: Baptized by John in the waters of the Jordan, this Judean peasant Jesus went forth, proclaiming God's present and imminent dominion of love. This teacher called forth children, women, and men to share and celebrate a new spirituality of love, a spiritual discipleship that embraced the praxis of equality for all people. And they baptized one another with the waters of life as a sign of a new and everlasting covenant of love with their God.

ALL: We join them today, celebrating that same covenant of love with our God. We ask you, loving and compassionate Mother, to bless these sacred gifts of water. (*Officiant(s) extends his/her hands over the water.*) May water's life-nurturing gifts connect us with your creation, your loving grace, and your dominion of peace. Amen.

Baptismal Covenant

(*Baptismal candidate(s) should respond after each question.*)

BAPTIZER(S): Do you embrace the God of unconditional love, who created life to be enjoyed and celebrated as a gift and a blessing, and do you promise to be co-creators of God's dominion of love?

CANDIDATE(S): I do.

BAPTIZER(S): Do you renounce all in the world that opposes the ethics of compassion, justice, and love, as taught by the historical Jesus of Nazareth?

CANDIDATE(S): I do.

BAPTIZER(S): Do you accept the responsibility as God's minister in the world to proclaim love, work for justice, and live a life of compassion for all peoples of the world and God's creation?

CANDIDATE(S): I do.

Rite of Baptism

BAPTIZER(S): N., *I/we* baptize you with these sacred waters of creation, and dedicate your life to the ministry of God's dominion of love in the name of our Mother God and Jesus of Nazareth. By the laying on of *my/our* hands, may the power and diverse gifts of God's spirit, the breath of life, fill you with joy and remain with you always. Amen.

REBAPTISM: A TRANSFORMING TIME

Jane Adams Spahr and *Kittredge Cherry*

Lesbian, gay, bisexual, and transgendered people who have felt rejected by their church of origin sometimes request rebaptism when they find a community of faith that welcomes them. Baptism as historically understood by the church is a sacrament, a rite instituted by Jesus to confer sanctifying grace and welcome into the community of faith. Even though rebaptism is not recognized by the institutional church, many people acknowledge it as a healing ritual of reclaiming all of oneself and God's grace. Baptism is usually once and for all time, but rebaptism may be appropriate in certain cases. Often those who seek rebaptism were originally baptized as children into a denomination that later condemned them—and in some cases excommunicated them—because of their sexual orientation. They tend to believe that their first baptism was invalidated by their church's exclusion of all of who they are. They may suffer from feelings of shame and a sense of being "dirty" due to society's heterosexism. Sometimes these feelings are compounded by childhood experiences of abuse and incest. These seekers long for "a sense of being brand-new." The ritual of rebaptism can move them significantly into further healing.

To prepare for rebaptism, the minister and the candidate meet for counseling sessions that cover many of the same issues as with an adult baptism: What does the church mean? What does baptism mean, historically and in the candidate's own life? Work together to create a ritual that will be meaningful. Instead of the baptismal vows in this liturgy, you may want to use the official baptism liturgy from the church of the candidate's childhood. Choose songs with water imagery. After the ritual, a party is a suitable way to celebrate a rebaptism.

(*Fifteen or twenty friends stand in a semicircle with the rebaptism candidate and minister at a lake, beach, river, or other body of water.*)

Greeting

MINISTER: Welcome to the rebaptism of N.! In the past, N. has felt that *s/he* could not be *herself/himself* in the church because *s/he* was a *lesbian/gay/ bisexual/transgendered person*. (*The minister or the candidate may retell the story of N.'s faith journey, focusing on the struggles and the joy that led to the rebaptism.*) Traditional baptism is a time of naming and welcoming. In this rebaptism, we recall that when Moses faced the burning bush and asked to know God's name, a voice from the fire replied, "I am who I am." God invites us to be who we are and to say, "Me, too!" We are what we are as lesbian, gay, bisexual, and transgendered people. Today N. is not ashamed to name both *her/his* sexual orientation and *her/his* faith. With this rebaptism, we affirm that N. is a new and wonderful creation, beloved by God and by this community.

Song

(*During the song, one or two friends fill a large bowl with water from the lake, river, or ocean and bring it back to the group.*)

Act of Rebaptism

MINISTER: This water is a symbol of your rebirth as a full member of God's beloved community. May this water wash away and help heal the memories that have separated you from God and from this gathered *community/church*. May this water wash away any feelings of worthlessness or shame. May this water quench your thirst for connection with the divine. May this water cleanse and purify your inner vision until you see only who you are as God's beloved. May this water remind you that you are strong, even when you feel weak, just as water has the strength to wear away stone; you will be rebaptized with the fluid strength that oppressed peoples have always used to wear down the stonehearted and the unjust.

N., do you open yourself to the Creator, Christ, and Holy Spirit, and desire a new life free of shame and fear? If so, respond by saying, "I do."

Will you live into love and justice, and will you be a faithful member of this gathered *community/church*? If so, respond by saying, "I promise, with the help of God."

N., I baptize you in the name of God, the Lover; Christ, the Beloved; and the Holy Spirit, which is Love in Action.

(*or*)

N., I baptize you in the name of Creator, Christ, and Holy Spirit.

Now I invite everyone here to take turns sharing from deep in your heart with N. to complete this rebaptism. Each person is asked to touch N. with water and speak to *her/him* about who *s/he* is to you and what *s/he* means to you. N. will respond by describing why you were chosen to share in this ritual. When you feel your turn is finished, conclude with the words, "N., you are truly a gift to me."

(*After everyone has had a chance to share with the candidate, the ritual continues.*)

Song

Final Blessing

MINISTER: Let us join hands to symbolize our connection with N., with each other, and with the source of life.

Creator God, together you and N. are recreating life anew. We are so grateful to be with N. at this significant moment of *her/his* life. It is an amazing experience to see the opening of N.'s heart to the people who love *her/him*. We thank you for the impact *s/he* makes on our lives. We are honored to be together to rebaptize *her/him* into this gathered *community/church* that loves and supports *her/him* as God created *her/him* to be.

Amen. Go forth in peace, joy, and wholeness!

BAPTISMAL LITURGY

James Lancaster

This rite is designed for inclusion in an ordinary worship service and is to be used for children of lesbian/gay people and lesbian and gay youth and adults. Pronouns are plural and in italics, and may be substituted with appropriate singular nouns as needed.

(*While the baptismal hymn or song is being sung, participants move to the baptismal font.*)

MINISTER: Baptism is the *rite/sacrament* through which we enter the Christian community and share in the body of Christ. Before beginning his own ministry, Jesus of Nazareth was baptized by John the Baptist. Today we gather to celebrate the baptism of N. (*if candidates are children and parents are sponsors*) *son/daughter* of N.

SPONSOR: *We* present N. to receive the gift of baptism.

(*If candidates are able to answer for themselves:*)

MINISTER: N., do you desire to be baptized?

CANDIDATE: I do.

ASSISTING MINISTER: Out of the primordial sea, divine Parent, you separated the waters from the waters and gave birth to our delicate, tender new world. In the dew of the sixth morning, our first parents took their first breaths from your life-giving nostrils and awoke to wonder, beauty, and perils unknown. You sustain and nourish the world and all its creatures through the gift of water.

(*If the candidate is a child:*)

ASSISTING MINISTER: Bless and inspire N. as *they* bring N. into the terrible beauty of our world, that *they* may raise and guide N. to love what is good and live for what is true.

(*If the candidate is an adult:*)

ASSISTING MINISTER: Bless and inspire N. as *they* enter new life as your *child/children* in the terrible beauty of our world, that *they* may be guided by you in wisdom, humor, and love.

MINISTER: In baptism we are cleansed in water and the Word of God. By these elements of God's loving mercy, we share in the creation of our world and the salvation of all peoples. We share in the salvation of Noah's family and the animals of the ark whom God brought safely through the flood. We share in the salvation of Moses, Miriam, and Aaron and all the Israelites whom God led through the waters of the sea out of the land of Egypt, that house of bondage. Through the peaceful waters of baptism God brought the early strife-torn Christian communities together. Today too God calls lesbian and gay people out of a hostile world into a new creation, a new day, life everlasting. In a thousand ways God brings us through perilous waters into the peaceful sea of God's love. N. has brought N. to our community to share in our fellowship, and in communion with God.

MINISTER (*addressing sponsors*): Do you promise to instruct N. in Christian life and our life together as a community of God, to support and nurture *them* in the Christian faith, and to share with *them* in *their* doubts, struggles, and joys?

SPONSOR: We do.

ASSISTING MINISTER: Let us pray. Gentle God, enliven the hearts, minds, and spirits of this community as we receive these new children of your loving grace, that the fullness of our lives may more richly bless each other. In your mercy,

CONGREGATION: Hear our prayer.

(*If the candidate is a child:*)

ASSISTING MINISTER: Ancient and ever-new Spirit, strengthen N. against the prejudice and oppression *they* will face as children of lesbian/gay parent(s). Navigate N. safely through the treacherous whirlpools of discrimination and the storms of homophobic hatred and ignorance, that *they* may learn to face these challenges with courage, love, and faith in your goodness. Fill N. with wisdom, understanding, and humor, that *they* may become more your loving children and more *their* own person, strong in self-respect and confident in the promises of your love. In your mercy,

CONGREGATION: Hear our prayer.

(*If the candidate is an adult:*)

ASSISTING MINISTER: Eternal Spirit who lives in our hearts, strengthen N. to live amid oppression, discrimination, and violence in a world that seems not to want us. Remind *them* that this is your world, created by you for N., and encourage N. as *they* seek to find strength and healing in your love, wisdom in your gentleness, and humor in the joy of your lovely world. In your mercy,

CONGREGATION: Hear our prayer.

(*Here the prayers of the people may be inserted.*)

MINISTER: Gracious Christ, we give you thanks for the power of your love, for the wonder of children, and for the happiness of fellowship. You shine with the clear vision of harmony and peace among all people: lesbian and gay, bisexual and straight, of all classes, all races, all faiths. You pour out the bright spirit of hope upon us. You separate the murky waters of ignorance and injury from the crystal-line waters of compassion and healing and nourish us with the water of new life. We join all the angels and the heavenly host in praising your glorious New Realm of eternal delight.

(*Minister motions for baptismal candidate to be held over the font or accompanies candidate into the baptismal pool. If so desired, parents may sprinkle their children at the font.*)

(*For each candidate:*)

MINISTER: N., this community baptizes you in the name of God, Creator (*water poured or candidate immersed*), Sustainer (*water poured or candidate immersed*), and Redeemer (*water poured or candidate immersed*). You are a new person, living in this world but partaking also of the new world yet to come.

CONGREGATION: Thanks be to God.

ASSISTING MINISTER: God of forever, our Heart, our Home, hasten the coming of your new creation and help us to live in this difficult and marvelous time with grace and dignity. Surround us with patience, inspirit us with indignation, comfort our grief and sorrow, enrapture us with passion, and lead us ever on to be more completely the people you have made us to be.

CONGREGATION: Amen.

(*A hymn may be sung and the service may be resumed.*)

THE MIXING OF OUR EARTH: A RITUAL FOR CREATING COMMUNITY

Sylvia Perez

This ritual is designed for use at a retreat both to introduce people and build community at the beginning and to provide a sense of closure at the end. Everyone planning to attend the retreat should be asked to bring along a handful of earth from near their home. The worship leader will also need to bring a large pot, a small tree, and tools for planting it.

At the Beginning of the Retreat

(*Everyone sits in a circle; a large pot is in the middle. A few gathering songs may be sung, and retreat leaders offer words of welcome.*)

WORSHIP LEADER: Each person here comes from a different place with *her/his* own unique stories, and all our stories are important. We recognize each other's individuality, just as we recognize the different types of soil surrounding our homes.

In a few minutes, we'll take turns placing the handfuls of earth that we've brought from home into this pot. We'll get fertile, rich soil from farming areas, clay from suburban properties, perhaps even earth from a potted plant in an urban apartment. (*The worship leader should adapt this list to include local soil conditions and name specific places. She or he may need to point out that anyone who forgot to bring soil from home can participate by getting a handful from the immediate area.*) When we mix these soils together, we have a new entity that is very different from our separate handfuls of earth. This new earth shares the strengths—and also the weaknesses—of the various soils that we bring.

Now I invite you to come forward one at a time as you feel moved and place your handful of earth into the pot. While you are doing that, say your name, tell us about where you come from, and make a short comment regarding your thoughts or expectations about this retreat.

(*After everyone has placed earth in the pot, the retreat leader speaks again.*)

WORSHIP LEADER: When we take different soils—moist and dry, light and dark, smooth and rocky—and mix them together, they become one soil. You can't tell where each different soil came from anymore. The earth in this pot is created here, right now.

Whatever feelings, memories, and hopes you bring with you to this retreat are now part of our mix too. They weave together here in God's presence to create a new community with all the unique qualities that each of us brings.

At the end of our retreat, we will use our earth to plant a tree here on our retreat site. In this way, our earth will continue to nurture life here in this place.

(*The gathering may end with song and/or a simple prayer.*)

At the End of the Retreat

(*People gather outside where the tree is to be planted. The hole for the tree can be dug in advance or the work incorporated into the ritual.*)

WORSHIP LEADER: We came to this retreat from many different places, each with our own unique emotions and experiences, each with a handful of earth from our particular home. We mixed our soil together. We became a new community.

Soon we will return to our homes, taking back with us new memories from our retreat together. We will also leave something behind: this tree, nurtured by the soil that we brought and blended here. We as lesbian and gay people are nurturers. Whether or not we have children, each one of us has the power to give life to other beings around us.

(*Place the tree in the hole.*)

I invite each of you, one by one, to take a handful of our earth and use it to plant this tree. As you do this, tell about what you experienced in this retreat.

(*After everyone has taken a turn, any remaining earth should be poured from the pot onto the ground near the newly planted tree. The ritual concludes as the tree is watered and everyone sings "Trees of the Field."*)

2

Rites
of Healing

By promoting sexism and homophobia, many religious institutions have directly contributed to the violence from which people seek healing. This is one reason violated persons sometimes turn away from religious institutions and turn to therapists and other professional healers. However, while professionals are important in healing, their services are often beyond the financial means of violated people. Moreover, they also frequently fail to address spiritual issues, including the sense of being alienated from and rejected by human communities of meaning. Thus healing from violence and illness demands a deeper liturgical dimension that enfolds violated, suffering persons in a supportive community of meaning and assures them of divine love.

Healing is one of the most ancient aspects of religion. Expressions of healing that integrate the physical, the psychic, and the spiritual are found throughout religious traditions. In healing rites, healing becomes a purification from death forces in the self and an opening up of the self to the healing life forces of creation and redemption. An essential aspect of healing is love communicated through touch.

INVOCATION OF REMEMBRANCE, HEALING, AND EMPOWERMENT IN A TIME OF AIDS

Elias Farajaje-Jonez

Opening Words

ONE: To the living and the dead, we bear witness. We gather in an act of remembrance of all our ancestors and in a particular way of all those lesbian, gay, bisexual, and transgendered people of color who have died in the struggle with AIDS, breast cancer, and ovarian cancer, but also of those who were denied adequate health care and were targets of racism, sexism, poverty, violence, homohatred, and other evils. Ours is a remembrance rooted in a spirit of solidarity and a spirit of resistance—a resistance that strengthens and empowers us to live and act boldly.

We make sacred space by forming a circle and purifying the space with earth, wind, water, and fire in honor of our Mother Earth who gives us life and to whom we return. We greet the four directions, and we invite our ancestors to be present with us, bringing their spirit of resistance. We pour libation, offering pure spring water to nurture the earth and our ancestors. As we do this, we will chant, "Those who have gone before us, rise up and call their names." We will hear their voices speak to us through a poem. Inspired by their voices, we will pledge our remembrance and our resistance. This is our healing of the pain of our losses. This is our self-empowerment as we create and claim the past, the present, and the future as our own, as we say, "Never again!"

(*Sacred space may be marked and grounded by playing a rain stick, ringing bells, burning incense, and/or sprinkling the ground with water and herbs such as mint.*)

Invocation of Ancestors

ONE: We know that as lesbian, gay, bisexual, and transgendered people of color, we have no future without our past, that we cannot hope to go forward without those who have gone before us, that we are not a minority but that all of us together are a majority. We now pour libation and invoke the presence of our ancestors. After each section, please join in the chant, "Those who have gone before us, rise up and call their names!"

It is our society's refusal to embrace otherness that has caused the situation in which we find ourselves today. If we lived in a world where the value of each individual's life was sacred, then we would not be witnesses to so much violence, pain, and destruction. But we live in a world in which our lives as lesbian, gay, bisexual, and transgendered people of color are perceived as expendable, in a society in which we can be exterminated without anyone really objecting.

If we have hope, it is hope tempered by memory and rage. Too often our capacity to forget has robbed us of the rage and anger that are rightfully ours, rage and anger that purify and transform, that change rather than kill and destroy. The shape of our world has been radically changed in light of the HIV/AIDS crisis. Whatever we do as we go forth from this place, whatever we say, whoever we are, let it be in solidarity with the oppressed and those who struggle for freedom throughout this country and throughout the world.

Not only do we invoke the presence of those oppressed for whatever reasons, but we also call upon our ancestors to be present here with us.

ALL: Those who have gone before us, rise up and call their names!

ONE: We call upon our Native American ancestors whose lands we invaded, who were massacred, yet who for more than five hundred years have resisted oppression, racism, and genocide. We call upon our sacred two-spirit ancestors who healed and drummed. We call upon them to be here, to open the way for us, to give us their permission and blessing to be here on their soil, near their waters.

ALL: Those who have gone before us, rise up and call their names!

ONE: We call upon the sixty-five million who perished in the middle passage, the forced migration of Afrikans to the Americas. We remember all those Afrikans who gave their lives to build the Americas. We ask them to be here with us.

ALL: Those who have gone before us, rise up and call their names!

ONE: We call upon our Latina and Latino ancestors who have struggled under Columbus's legacy of destruction and death. We call upon them to be present with us, bringing their spirit of resistance.

ALL: Those who have gone before us, rise up and call their names!

ONE: We call upon the many Asian and Pacific Islander sisters and brothers who lost their lives in building Gold Mountain, who perished in concentration camps here, who have struggled to keep their sacred lands. We call upon them to be with us.

ALL: Those who have gone before us, rise up and call their names!

ONE: We call upon our Arab ancestors, those who have been exiled and died struggling for their homelands. We ask them to be present with us.

ALL: Those who have gone before us, rise up and call their names!

ONE: We call upon the eleven million Jews, anarchists, queer women and men, people of color, Gypsies, people with disabilities who were exterminated during the Nazi Holocaust. We ask these ancestors to strengthen us with their presence.

ALL: Those who have gone before us, rise up and call their names!

ONE: And now, as we invoke the presence of Hattie Mae Cohens, Patrick Red Elk, and Brian Mock, our sisters and brothers, and all who through the ages have been killed by homohatred, we call upon our ancestors, our lovers, partners, life-companions, and friends who are no longer visibly present to us, but the presence of whose spirits allows us to live. We remember those women lost to breast cancer and ovarian cancer, and those women and men who have died in our holocaust, the AIDS pandemic. Let us call out the names of our ancestors, new and old.

ALL: Those who have gone before us, rise up and call their names!

ONE: May they walk with us and bring us new strength for the struggle. May they tenderly wipe the tears from our eyes. May they guide us to see that, as lesbian, gay, bisexual, and transgendered people of color, our walk is together. May they remind us that we are the tribes of the moon, a sacred people.

Affirmation

ALL:

> Yes, we honor you, our sisters and brothers.
> Yes, we will remember and recognize you who have gone before us.
> Without you, we would not exist here today.
> Through us, you live on from generation to generation, from everlasting to everlasting.
> And so we commit ourselves to a spirit of resistance and life.
> We raise our light, our lives, our hope, our love, and we say boldly and without fear, ''Never again!''

A HEALING SERVICE

A. Stephen Pieters

Prelude

Call to Worship

(*May be read by two readers or responsively.*)

27

ONE: We come together to worship you, O God, our Great Physician.

ALL: Jesus healed the man with the withered arm.

ONE: Some of us come here with cancer, heart disease, or other conditions that threaten our lives.

ALL: Jesus healed Simon's mother-in-law.

ONE: Some of us are sick from alcoholism and drug abuse.

ALL: Jesus healed the lepers.

ONE: Some of us hope for healing of depression or emotional problems.

ALL: Jesus healed the man with an unclean spirit.

ONE: Some of us need healing from abuse.

ALL: Jesus healed the woman with the twelve-year hemorrhage.

ONE: Some of us look for healing from HIV, AIDS, and related infections.

ALL: Jesus healed the man born blind.

ONE: Whatever the condition of our lives, we trust you, O God, to touch us and to heal us through the power of the Risen Christ.

ALL: We dare to come for healing, here and now!

ONE: And so we sing to you, Amazing God, because you have shown us, through Jesus Christ, that you are greater than any disease or condition that keeps us from being fully alive.

Hymn of Praise

Prayer of Confession

We come to you, our Loving and Healing Parent, remembering the miracles of healing from Jesus' time. We confess that sometimes we think of miracles as something that happened only long ago and far away. We admit our scientific skepticism. We recognize that our hopes for healing are often plagued by crises of faith. And sometimes, God, we're simply scared of how our lives would change if we were healed. Help us to willingly suspend our disbelief! Give us the faith to claim the healing you would have us enjoy. Help us to see your healing grace in every day of our lives, even in our dying. Open our hearts to the healing warmth of your presence.

Assurance of Forgiveness

Readings

Suggested readings: Psalm 30; Mark 5:25–34

Offering

Offertory Anthem

Doxology

Sermon

Rite of Healing

(*At this point in the service, those who are offering prayers for healing will station themselves in front of the altar or around the sides of the sanctuary, if room is needed. Each minister of healing may have one or two attendants who will also lay on hands and be ready to support the person who has come for healing. Some may wish for anointing with oil. Others may simply want the laying on of hands. During this time of prayer, contemplative music is appropriate. Some congregations may wish to sing hymns softly.*)

Closing Hymn

Benediction

As we go from here, let us remember what Jesus told the woman with the twelve-year hemorrhage: "Your faith has made you whole. Go in peace." In the name of God who creates us, the Christ who sets us free, and the Spirit who makes us one. Amen!

Postlude

RITE OF HEALING FROM LIFE-THREATENING DISEASE

Zalmon Sherwood

When a friend develops a life-threatening disease, such as cancer or AIDS, the best response is quiet, personal, and unpublicized assistance. The friend or colleague who works silently and efficiently behind the scenes to help with anything that requires attending becomes a beloved saint in the eyes of the sick person and his or her loved ones. When visiting someone who is extremely ill, a peppy, upbeat approach is inappropriate. Just be there by his or her side, quietly talking when the person feels like it and remaining silent when the person is tired or is dozing off. Hold the patient's hand. Don't be afraid to touch or kiss him or her. If you are able to offer some form of religious comfort, and if the patient is open to receiving it, by all means do it.

When you have a friend with AIDS, make sure that as he or she weakens, someone is coordinating necessary care. If a lover is nursing the ill person, give that person a much-needed break and take over for a couple of hours. If the patient is alone, when conditions worsen and the person becomes weaker, make sure that someone is preparing meals, bathing him or her, and keeping his or her place clean. A grave illness is no time for abandonment, but rather a time for patience and solid support.

With the patient's permission, a small group of friends may gather to offer prayers and a brief, simple rite of healing. Gifts of fragrant flowers, herbs, and perfumed oils may be offered during the rite.

(Friends gather around the ill person's bed, lightly touch some part of his or her body, and pray silently until one is moved to offer a prayer, such as those that follow.)

ONE: We feel so sad to see our sister N. hurting, confined to this bed. We are with you in your struggle: each and every day we will be by your side, providing you with loving and tender care, memories of good times shared, hope for restored health and activity.

OR

ONE: Great Healing Spirit, strengthen our friend's resolve to live. Deliver him from illness, restore his laughter, hope, and delight in running, playing and sharing life.

OR

ONE: We're angry that our brother N. has AIDS.
Our first impulse is to deny what is happening,
or to refuse to believe that
our strong, handsome, talented friend
is suffering from the ignorance and bigotry of others.
We long to embrace you, brother, to protect you
from the horror and indignity,
to strengthen our commitment
to caring and advocacy.
All we have to offer is our selfishness and cowardice,
but there is hope that we might learn from
the example of your courage,
the beauty of your spirit,
the power of your love that burns fiercely inside us.

(The following litany may be recited by the group.)

READER: Goddess of grace, you nurture us with a love deeper than we know, and your will for us is healing and salvation.

ALL: Goddess of love, you enter into our lives, our pain, and our brokenness, and you stretch out your healing hands to us wherever we are.

READER: Goddess of strength, you fill us with your presence and send us forth in love and healing among those we meet.

ALL: Touch and heal our bodies suffering from sickness, injury, and disability, and make us whole again.

READER: Touch and heal our minds from confusion and doubt.

ALL: Touch and heal our hearts burdened by anguish, despair, and isolation, and set us free in love.

READER: Break the bonds of our imprisonment to fear, compulsion, and addiction.

ALL: Give us liberty from old hurts and painful memories.

READER: Fill us with peace in our grief from separation and loss.

ALL: Work through all who share in your ministry of healing, and renew us in compassion and strength.

READER: We pray for courage to walk with those who are living with HIV. Encourage our hearts and open our hands.

ALL: We pray for those who are afflicted with HIV and with any other grief or trouble. Give us relief and quietness of spirit.

READER: We pray for all HIV caregivers, hospital workers, and research-ers. Be with them in their tasks, enliven their spirits.

ALL: We pray for the loved ones, friends, and families of persons living with HIV. Fill them with your healing and redemptive love.

READER: We pray for those who have died of AIDS and for all the departed.

ALL: May angels surround them and saints welcome them in peace.

READER: We pray for the frightened, the timid, and for those who breed fear.

ALL: Loosen our bonds and empower us in the work of liberation.

(*A period of silence is followed by a concluding prayer.*)

READER: Holy and Life-giving Breath, fill us with your love; comfort our sisters and brothers living with AIDS. Open our hearts to provide for their needs, to take away their isolation, to share their journey of suffering and sorrow, as well as hope and joy, and to be present with them in their dying, that no one need suffer or die alone. Remove fear, prejudice, and hatred from our midst. Breathe on us, fill us to overflowing with the fire of your passion for justice. Make love with us once more, and heal.

A LITANY FOR DIALOGUE AMONG
PEOPLE WITH DIFFERENT SEXUAL ORIENTATIONS

Eric H. F. Law

Opening Words

ONE: Dear brothers and sisters in Christ: We gather here at this time and place to pray and to talk with each other about our commonalities and differences. Throughout the history of the church, conflict among members of the body of Christ has been common and sometimes inevitable: conflict among Jesus' disciples, disputes between Peter and Paul, controversy over whether Gentiles can be Christians, and disagreement about which books to include in Christian scriptures, just to name a few. They are part of what it means to live in any diverse community. As Christians, we have Jesus Christ, our great mediator and reconcilor, who teaches us to love our neighbor as ourselves and to love our enemies. If we commit ourselves to the dialogue and reconciliation process, we believe we will discover the full meaning of living in Christ's community where truth and justice can be found for all.

A Litany for Dialogue

ONE: Let us pray:

O God, you made us in your own image: with eyes to see, ears to listen, mouths to speak, and hearts to feel. Through Jesus, you have shown us how to see and perceive, listen and discern, speak and illuminate, and feel and be moved with compassion.

Help us to realize that we are not here to debate who is right and who is wrong, but to experience true dialogue in which we strive to communicate honestly and listen actively and openly to each other.

(*Pause for silence*)

God in your mercy,

ALL: Hear our prayer.

ONE: Give us the wisdom to recognize our preconceived assumptions and perceptions about others—some are conscious; some are unconscious. Make us aware of how our assumptions influence the way we listen and interpret others' words and actions and how they affect the way we speak and act in the group.

(*Silence*)

God in your mercy,

ALL: Hear our prayer.

ONE: Open our hearts and minds to experience new ideas, feelings, situations, and people, even though at times the process may be uncomfortable.

(*Silence*)

God in your mercy,

ALL: Hear our prayer.

ONE: Give us the strength to take responsibility for what we say and what we say on behalf of a group. Inspire us to speak with words that others can hear and understand, and with eloquence to reveal the truth.

(*Silence*)

God in your mercy,

ALL: Hear our prayer.

ONE: Expand our listening ability to include not just words, but all the ways that humankind communicates: through feelings, body language, and different kinds of silence.

(*Silence*)

God in your mercy,

ALL: Hear our prayer.

ONE: Give us the courage to take responsibility for our own feelings as they surface. We know that feelings may be triggered by particular words or actions, but they may or may not be directly related to the particular interaction. Help us find ways to communicate our feelings without blaming others so that we can constructively hear and learn the consequences of each other's words and actions.

(*Silence*)

God in your mercy,

ALL: Hear our prayer.

ONE: Keep us under the shadow of your wings and help us respect one another by holding the personal information shared here in confidence, because only in this way can we feel free to say what is in our minds and hearts.

(*Silence*)

God in your mercy,

ALL: Hear our prayer.

ONE: Forgive our sins as we forgive those who sin against us, and take away the arrogance and hatred that infect our hearts.

(*Silence*)

God in your mercy,

ALL: Hear our prayer.

ONE: Break down the walls that separate us; unite us in bonds of love; and work through our struggle and confusion to accomplish your purposes on earth; that, in your good time, all people may serve you in harmony as one body; through Jesus Christ our great reconciler and mediator.

ALL: Amen.

RITE OF HEALING
FROM LESBIAN/GAY BASHING

Zalmon Sherwood

This rite is designed for those who have suffered from the violence of lesbian/gay bashing. It seeks to repudiate this violence to and violation of sexual minorities.

READER: We come together particularly in mourning and healing for our sister, N., who has suffered violence from lesbian bashers, who has decided to resist it, who seeks the healing of her soul, her mind, and her body from its poisons and blows. We join her in standing firm against such senseless cruelty. We reject its legal sanctions, its cultural acceptance, and its religious cover-up. We cry out against it. We pledge ourselves to make it visible. It must be stopped. Here, in this place, it will be stopped.

We are a gentle people, committed to peace and justice. And yet our very existence is an affront to people who strike out against us in ignorance and hatred, filling our lives with fear.

ALL: My God, my God, why have you abandoned us? We have cried desperately for help, but still it does not come. During the day we call you, but you do not answer. We call at night, but get no rest.

READER: The negative images bombard us. We read headlines that twist the truth and distort our lives; we are invaded by radio announcers who tell cruel jokes and invite callers to rage against our relationships; we watch television and movies that portray us as fools and psychopaths, stereotypes that incite violence against us.

ALL: We are not treated like real persons, but regarded as worms, despised and scorned by many. Those who see us make fun of us; they stick out their tongues and shake their heads. And eventually, they strike.

READER: First, the obscene calls that disturb our rest. Then the threatening hate mail, followed by malicious graffiti and slashed tires. The vicious rumors circulate, and soon people everywhere regard us as monsters, witches, faggots to be burned.

ALL: It was you who brought us safely through birth, and when we were babies, you kept us safe. We have relied on you. Do not stay away from us! Trouble is near, and there is no one to help.

READER: Preachers, teachers, employers, parents make groundless charges against us. We have been slapped for saying something about politics or religion, for having a different view about loving, for crying. We have been threatened when we refuse to do something we are told to do.

ALL: Our enemies surround us like fierce bulls. They open their mouths like lions, roaring and tearing at us.

READER: We are shoved and when we do not run, we are beaten. What do we mean by beaten? We mean that parts of our bodies have been hit violently and repeatedly, resulting in painful bruises, swelling, bleeding wounds, unconsciousness. Few people have ever seen our swollen faces and broken bodies, because we stayed indoors afterward, feeling afraid and ashamed.

ALL: Our strength is gone, gone like water spilled on the ground. All our bones are out of joint. Our hearts are like melted wax. Our throats are dry as dust. You have left us for dead. My God, my God, why have you abandoned us?

(*A period of silence follows.*)

READER: We have heard the anguish of lesbians and gay men. We have cried out to God with lamentation and tears, but we have not been heard. We have been forsaken, abandoned, left alone in humiliation, guilt, despair. Too often the victim herself has been made to feel that she is the cause of the problem. We must begin anew. We must forge ahead to unlock the wellsprings of justice, healing, hope, and liberation. Let us invite our sister to tell her story.

(*The battered woman may choose to give an account of the assault, the history of violence against her, the things that locked her into this situation, and how she has begun to resist and seek freedom and a new life. She may prefer to remain silent. Several friends might surround the woman and silently anoint parts of her body with perfumed ointment.*)

READER: Our bodies were created to feel and enjoy life. They have been made the objects of violence and the seat of pain. Woman, throw off this pain. Cast off this humiliation. Be healed.

(*The battered woman stands and joins in a circle with the community. Together they say:*)

ALL: We are here to end the violence. Yes, we will!
We are here to break the terror. Yes, we will!
We are here to heal the wounded. Yes, we will!
We are here to help each other. Yes, we will!
We are here to change the system. Yes, we will!

READER:
We offer our prayers on behalf of all who are abused.
For children who suffer at the hands of parents;
for spouses, beaten and destroyed by the one who promised to love them forever;
for all people ignored, harassed, cheated, hated.
Let all who are oppressed no longer remain passive victims of violence,
but act courageously to end all abuse, all bashings that cripple our lives.

ALL: We are moving out together. Yes, we are!
We are creating a new world that is safe and happy. Yes, we are!
Where women, men, and children can live together without fear. Yes, we will!
The end of the old, the beginning of the new. This is the time!
The end of terror, the beginning of safety. This is the place!
The end of silence. The beginning of protest and change.
We are the ones, and we will do it. Yes, we will!

RITE OF HEALING FROM RAPE

Zalmon Sherwood

Rape is usually associated with acts of aggression, hostility, and violence by men toward women. Lesbians have been assaulted and violated by straight men as a most brutal form of harassment and rape. Rape also occurs between women and between men. The following rite was designed for a small group of gay men inside a prison, where rape is rarely a sexual act but one of violence, politics, and acting out of power roles. Straight prisoners regard gay prisoners as "women who are asking for it." This attitude is directly parallel to that of the female rape victim, who is often accused of "asking for it."

The gay prisoner must face a horrible decision: to live independently, thus making himself a target of sexual intimidation, assault, and rape; or to live subserviently, paying for protection by sexually servicing prisoners who have a high propensity for hostility and violence; or to live in protective custody, that is, in segregation or solitary confinement, which denies the gay prisoner access to recreational and educational programs and to the few privileges available to other prisoners. The cumulative psychological effects of sensory deprivation from long periods of solitary confinement are devastating.

(*This healing rite begins with the man who was raped joining hands with his friends to form a circle. Someone in the group says:*)

ONE: We are here because our brother N. has been violated. His body, his feelings, and his spirit have all been gravely injured. We are here to mourn with him and also to cry out in anger with him. We are outraged—outraged at the hostility to gay men and the distortion of sexuality into violence that are all around us, taking the most extreme form in rape. We are filled with grief because we don't know when the violence will end and how we can repair the damage that has been done. But we refuse to give up. We will not be defeated. We will not be intimidated and turned into fearful people unable to claim the little freedom we have inside these walls. Locked into this cruel, predatory, nightmarish situation, we cling to a desperate need to feel strong, worthwhile, and in control.

ALL: You have been hurt so deeply, N.,
    you cannot trust.
    You cannot love or hate.
    All feelings have been replaced
    by a cold detachment.
    Never will we, your friends,
    allow such searing pain again.
    Let us lead you from this unutterable sorrow
    to a place where violence and fear are banished.

(*After a period of silence, the man may choose to say something about his experience, or he may prefer to remain silent.*)

READER: We love and affirm our brother N. who has been hurt.
    Although he has been injured, he is not destroyed.

Although he has been demeaned, he has not lost his integrity.
Although he has been subjected to ugliness, he is still handsome.
Although evil has gripped him, yet he is still good.
Although lies may seek to impugn him, yet he is still truthful.
We affirm his wholeness, his goodness, his truthfulness, his
    integrity, his beauty. We dispel the forces of destruction, of
    ugliness, of violence, and of lies that seek to make him their
    victim.

(*The friends gather around the man who was raped. They gently place their hands on the man as a symbol of healing.*)

ALL: There are frightened persons who teach us to hate ourselves,
    who consider our lives worthless, who wish us harm.
    Only our love for each other can heal the illness
    of their coldhearted will.
    From violence to your body, N., be healed.
    From violence to your feelings, N., be healed.
    From violence to your mind and spirit, N., be healed.
    Feel our love that surrounds you, upholds you, flows through you,
        caresses you, and wills you to be whole.
    Be whole, brother, be whole.

LITANY OF AFFIRMATION

Colleen Darraugh

ONE: It is not we who have chosen God, but God who has chosen us.
    And we are affirmed as we hear the voice of God say:
ALL: I will make of the outcasts a strong nation (Micah 4:7).
ONE: Many of us—gay, lesbian, bisexual, and transgendered—have
    experienced exclusion, rejection, alienation, and hopelessness, but
    we have heard the voice of God say:
ALL: I will make of the outcasts a strong nation.
ONE: Many of us—differently abled, hearing-impaired, and heterosex-
    ual with so-called different or unacceptable relationships or fami-
    lies—have experienced the inaccessibility and inhospitality of many
    churches, synagogues, and temples, but we have heard the voice of
    God say:
ALL: I will make of the outcasts a strong nation.
ONE: Many of us have felt silenced, unheard, dismissed because of our
    language, culture, race, or gender, but in our own languages and
    in the midst of our life experiences we have heard the voice of God say:

38

ALL: I will make of the outcasts a strong nation.

ONE: Many of us have been treated as outcasts as we have lived with and through sexual, physical, and emotional abuse, HIV, breast cancer, and other life-threatening illnesses, but we have heard the voice of God say:

ALL: I will make of the outcasts a strong nation.

ONE: It is not we who have chosen God, but God who has chosen us, and we are affirmed as we hear the voice of God say:

ALL: I will make of the outcasts a strong nation.

CEREMONY OF DISSOLUTION

James Lancaster

This ceremony is designed to be a simple dissolution of a marital bond between two women or two men. It is not designed to castigate them for any perceived or imagined failure, to elicit confessions, or to bestow forgiveness. Any hymns or prayers to that effect are inappropriate to this ceremony.

The vows will be discussed beforehand between the individuals and the minister as part of the counseling that should precede this dissolution ceremony, in the same way that counseling precedes a holy union. The ribbon symbolizing the dissolution may be of different colors or types if the participants so choose. Practicing the ritual untying is advised lest the ribbons knot embarrassingly during the ceremony.

Hymn

ASSISTING MINISTER: "Yahweh said to Abram, 'Leave your country, your family, and your parents' house, for the land I will show you. . .' So Abram went as Yahweh told him. . . . Abram was seventy-five years old when he left Haran." Thanks be to God.

CONGREGATION: Amen.

MINISTER: Today we are called to witness the start of a journey. After great struggle, thought, and prayer, N. and N. have decided to dissolve their union. Each gives back to the other the life that was shared, and henceforth they shall lead separate lives. Although their road to this day has been fraught with deep pain as well as great joy, they have chosen to end their relationship not in bitterness or in flight, but as *sisters/brothers,* in Christian love and the remembrance of love. Many of us have known and grown to love them as a couple. We gather here at the start of this new journey to celebrate their life together and bless them for their lives apart.

ASSISTING MINISTER: Let us pray. God of all people, we often leave what is familiar and safe and come to places strange to us, where friends are few and the horizon bleak. Yet in the wilderness you sent ravens with food for the prophet Elijah. You sent manna from heaven to feed the children of Israel. In the wilderness you sent angels to minister to your child, Jesus Christ. Strengthen us to be angels to our friends, N. and N., that we may comfort and sustain them through this painful time. In the love that you spread like light over all the earth, we pray.

CONGREGATION: Amen.

Silence for Individual Reflection and Prayer

ASSISTING MINISTER: A reading from . . . (*Suggested lessons are Matt. 12:1–8, Matt. 6:25–34, Luke 6:36–38, Luke 11:9–13, Isa. 11:6–9, and Psalm 121. These lessons should not be to punish but to strengthen all the congregation; they may warn against sitting in judgment of others.*)

Homily

Hymn

MINISTER (*motions for the participants to come before the altar*): N. and N., your journey has been long, and now, like Abram, like Sarai, you face another long journey. This community has gathered to give thanks to God for your life together and for the life you have shared with us. Yet while that union has ended, you remain a part of their community, sheltered in its arms and loved in its hearts. We grieve for the sorrow of this loss, for it is a loss to us as well as to you. But just as the promise of resurrection follows the death of someone dearly loved and gives us hope and joy, so the promise of new life for each of you and for this community shines like dawn upon this day. The new lives we will share together shall be no less filled with grace and beauty than those that came before. We strengthen and uphold each other to be able to receive that grace and that beauty.

Will the congregation please rise? (*The congregation rises.*)

When N. and N. were joined in holy union, they made vows and promises to each other. This congregation stood witness to their union. Today as we dissolve that union, we speak of responsibilities on this solemn occasion as well.

MINISTER (*addressing one participant*): Do you, N., promise to forgive what needs to be forgiven, and to ask God to strengthen you for forgiveness? Do you promise to cherish the memory of this relationship, to reflect upon it, to learn and grow from the mistakes that were made, and to be heartened by the good things you gave to each other?

PARTICIPANT: I do.

MINISTER (*addressing the other participant*): Do you, N., promise to forgive what needs to be forgiven, and to ask God to strengthen you for forgiveness? Do you promise to cherish the memory of this relationship, to reflect upon it, to learn and grow from the mistakes that were made, and to be heartened by the good things you gave to each other?

PARTICIPANT: I do.

MINISTER (*addressing the congregation*): Does this assembled community promise to uphold these *sisters/brothers* in love and kindness? Do we promise to nurture our relationships with each of them, sharing laughter as well as tears? Do we promise to reflect upon our own experiences and learn from them new ways of being ever more loving children of God?

CONGREGATION: We do.

(*Assistant Minister brings forth loosely tied ribbons and holds them between the participants. The minister may say the following words or the ritual may be performed wordlessly, in silence or accompanied by music.*)

MINISTER: The ribbon symbolizes the union of your lives. Today you give those lives back to each other.

(*The participants gently pull the ribbons apart, and then exchange the ribbons.*)

MINISTER (*raising hands in blessing and addressing the participants*): May the sweetness of your time together rise like fresh spring air in your memory. May the angry words and hurtful deeds fall away from you like ash that is blown away. May each day bring you solace and joy, and each night, comfort and rest. May you feel God's gentle hands beneath and about you, and may you know that you are loved.

Moment of Silence

MINISTER: You are free to live your lives in the fullness of God's gifts and in the mercy of life in Christ. This community affirms its love for you, even as we share that love with each other.

Sharing of the Peace

(*After the sharing of the peace, the participants may return to their seats in the congregation.*)

ASSISTING MINISTER: Let us pray. We thank you, Sovereign of the Ages, for your deep and abiding love for us. We ask that you carry us on your wings through times of trial, that we may not be caught in the tempter's snares. We pray that you guide us in your way of peace and catch us up in your robe of wonder, that we may know only your love, and nothing but your love, forevermore. In your holy name, we pray.

CONGREGATION: Amen.

ASSISTING MINISTER: Go in peace. Serve God.

CONGREGATION: Thanks be to God.

Hymn

3

Funerals and
Memorial Services

Dying is no more a purely individual act than living is. Like every great milestone in life, death is celebrated by a ceremony whose purpose is to express the individual's solidarity with family and community.

So often people attend antiseptic funerals that cover up suffering. People who cannot share their pain cannot truly worship together. Yet funeral and memorial rites should not be opportunities for grandiose tributes that include tasteless gimmicks meant to manipulate grief. Rather, they are critical times in which people are called to pause, to gather, and to lament a particular loss to the community.

The AIDS pandemic has forced the gay and lesbian community to become very familiar with death and dying. For example, Metropolitan Community Church of San Francisco performs approximately one hundred fifty funerals a year, most of them for gay men who died of AIDS without any church affiliation. Those in the church have learned that grief is expressed in many ways. One funeral service, for example, was planned in advance by the deceased, who insisted that after the service each mourner was to hurl one of his prized Fiestaware plates into a fireplace to release his or her anger. People in this community have also come to see that the grieving process may begin with other kinds of rites, such as a marriage ceremony conducted while one or both partners is near death.

Perhaps the lesbian and gay community's most fitting model for a memorial service is the ritual involved in the Names Project AIDS Memorial Quilt. Many people with AIDS have opted not to plan any kind of public funeral, but have instead asked friends to design a three-by-six-foot panel for the quilt. The panels memorialize the lost ones, offer hope to those who are living, honor those who have made a difference, and motivate those who have yet to join the fight against AIDS. It is not the thousands of panels alone that move people, but also the dignified manner in which the quilt is exhibited in school gymnasiums, convention centers, museums, and other public spaces. To view the quilt is to walk on holy ground, to listen quietly to the endless litany of the names of the dead, to watch in awe as each panel is carefully, reverently, gracefully unfolded. This is liturgy in its purest, most sacred form.

The following rites are offered to assist people in honoring the dead while bearing witness to the hope and continuing work of the community, realizing that life is fragile and that none of us is here forever.

TELLING LOVE'S STORY:
REMEMBERING AND RESPONDING TO AIDS

Diann L. Neu

For the last decade HIV/AIDS has haunted the world. Each of us must grapple with this epidemic and respond with love, compassion, and support. AIDS is the plague of our era. The Names Project AIDS Memorial Quilt reminds us profoundly that we walk amid life and death daily.

World AIDS Day, December 1, offers an opportune occasion to hold this sacred event. The ritual was created by our women-church group the week the Names Quilt came to Washington, D.C. We named our beloved ones, told their stories, shed many tears, and shared our hopes. Use this ritual as a model for the one your group needs to share. Such an event may be the first time your community openly confronts the HIV/AIDS crisis and the issues that surface because of it. Be sensitive, compassionate, and bold.

Preparing to Celebrate

Gather candles, red ribbons, and straight pins to give to each participant. Also provide a large candle, a loaf of bread, and a glass of water. Place them on a cloth that is significant for the occasion. (We used a blanket that belonged to our dead friend, Shawn Sheffield, who was born HIV-positive, lived with the AIDS virus, and died of AIDS at the age of five. On his blanket, we placed pictures of Shawn's quilt panel that several of us had helped create.)

Naming the Circle

ONE: Welcome to this place of remembrance. During this time together we will focus on "Telling Love's Story: Remembering and Responding to AIDS." Think of those you know who are living with HIV and AIDS, those who have died of AIDS-related causes, those who have been affected by HIV and AIDS. Let's create our sacred circle by sharing our name and the names of those we remember, and then honor them by pinning ourselves with a red ribbon.

(*Members of the group share names.*)

Calling to Gather

(*One person continues by lighting the larger candle from the small one and then begins to speak.*)

ONE: These beloved ones are with us in this circle now. Remembering them reminds us that we are all people living with AIDS—those we have just named, those who have lost loved ones, those who care for them, and every one of us struggling to eradicate this disease. AIDS has changed our lives.

Our beloved friends carry or carried in their bodies this debilitating disease. Some have been discriminated against; most have been loved deeply. Each has surely felt anger and pain, hope and fear, support and loneliness. They are here with us now reminding us how we must respond to AIDS: with love, tears, rage, compassion, and hope.

One response is the Names Project AIDS Memorial Quilt that has blanketed malls, fields, and gymnasiums across the United States with thousands of fabric, coffin-sized panels, each bearing the name of someone killed by AIDS. The AIDS quilt is a monument to those we have loved and lost. It is a monument that shows leaders of every government they must respond to AIDS by granting money for research. It is a monument that shows people of every nation and neighborhood that we must unite, remember, and respond now.

How are we responding to AIDS? Our gathering tonight is a response. Let us quiet ourselves and remember.

Singing Together

"They Are Falling All Around Me," by Bernice Johnson Reagon, from *B'lieve I'll Run On,* © 1975

Listening to a Reading

"Face of AIDS" from *A Shallow Pool of Time,* by Fran Peavey, a woman living with AIDS

Sharing a Response

ONE PERSON: Let us respond together.
ALL: We know the face of AIDS. We are here, right here in your midst.
LEFT SIDE: We are friends, partners, lovers, family, neighbors.
ALL: We know the face of AIDS. We are here, right here in your midst.
RIGHT SIDE: We are caresharers, justice workers, health care professionals, social workers, ministers.
ALL: We know the face of AIDS. We are here, right here in your midst.
LEFT SIDE: We are students, teachers, parents, sisters, and brothers.

ALL: We know the face of AIDS. We are here, right here in your midst.

RIGHT SIDE: Some of us are wise elders; some are caring adults; some are searching youth; some are wonder-filled children.

ALL: We know the face of AIDS. We are here, right here in your midst.

LEFT SIDE: Some of us are lesbian; some of us are gay; some of us are straight; some of us are bisexual.

ALL: We know the face of AIDS. We are here, right here in your midst.

RIGHT SIDE: Some of us have AIDS or might get it.

ALL: We know the face of AIDS. We are here, right here in your midst.

LEFT SIDE: Some of us feel angry and sad, fearful and fragile, vulnerable and alone.

ALL: We know the face of AIDS. We are here, right here in your midst.

RIGHT SIDE: We are a multicolored and many-cultured people: black, brown, yellow, white, red.

ALL: We know the face of AIDS. We are here, right here in your midst.

LEFT SIDE: All of us are people of faith, awaiting the day when AIDS is a distant memory.

ALL: We know the face of AIDS. We are here, right here in your midst.

ONE PERSON: What else shall we add to this litany? Tell us and we will respond.

(*At this point, spontaneous offerings from individuals may be affirmed by the group response.*)

Listening to a Song

ANOTHER: Let's listen to "The Letter" by Ruben Blades, sung by Holly Near on *Sky Dances* (© 1988).

Listening to a Poem

ANOTHER: I will read "The Concert" by Ken Cierpial, who died with AIDS October 23, 1992.

> for my soulmate, Bob Canavello
> I have learned how to learn,
> How to read,
> How to practice.
>
> But today I am getting ready for my life's performance
> By forgetting everything I know
> And letting everything go.

Look! How I am now dancing between the notes
Of the music that my soul plays!

Sharing Together

ONE (*after a pause*): AIDS affects us all and takes us to places where we
would dare not go. How are you affected by AIDS? What love story do
you tell? What would you want on your quilt panel when you die?

Let's reflect on these questions for a few minutes alone in quiet.
(*Pause.*)

Let's gather with two or three others to share our reflections.
(*Participants share.*)

Let's close our sharing now by bringing ourselves back to the larger
circle.

Prayers of the Faithful

ONE PERSON: Compassionate Holy One, open our hearts and minds and
hands so that we may connect ourselves to the global community of
others responding to AIDS as we pray:

We remember all the women, men, and children in this country
and around the world who are living with AIDS.

ALL: Justice demands that we remember and respond.

ONE: We remember all who care for people living and dying with AIDS in
their homes, in hospices, and in support centers.

ALL: Justice demands that we remember and respond.

ONE: We remember all who are involved in research and hospital care
that they may respect the dignity of each person.

ALL: Justice demands that we remember and respond.

ONE: We remember all partners who are left mourning for their
beloved ones.

ALL: Justice demands that we remember and respond.

ONE: We remember all parents who learn the truth of their children's
lives through their process of facing death.

(*At this point, spontaneous offerings from individuals may be affirmed by the
group response.*)

Sharing of Bread and Water

(*One person picks up the bread, another the water.*)

ONE: We remember by blessing bread and water, symbols of nourishment and thirst. Let us stand and place our hands on this bread and this water.

OTHER: Blessed are you, Nourishing One, for giving us bread to strengthen us for the long journey. May its healing power rise within us.

ONE: Blessed are you, Thirst Quencher, for giving us water to keep us alive in the desert. May its life-giving power flow through us.

OTHER: As we eat and drink let us remember.

(*Participants eat and drink.*)

Lighting of Candles

(*One person takes a small candle, lights it from the large one, circles it around the large one, and speaks.*)

ONE: I light a candle of [e.g., *hope*]. Come, take a candle, light it, saying, "I light a candle of [e.g., *forgiveness/thanks/sorrow*]."

(*Candle lighting and sharing continue.*)

Praying a Prayer of Hope

(*After all candles are lighted, she continues.*)

ONE: We bring together many candles, many lights.
As those who keep the night watch await the dawn,
We remain vigilant,
Until a cure for AIDS is found,
Until those dying with AIDS are comforted,
Until truth sets us free,
Until love drives out injustice.
We shall not give up the fight.

Singing Together

"We Shall Not Give Up the Fight," a South African freedom song

Greeting of Peace

ONE: Not giving up is hard and exhausting work. We need all the hugs we can get. Receive an embrace for all that may be required of you in remembering and responding to AIDS. (*Group members hug one another.*)

Sending Forth

ONE: Let us open our circle of support and compassion now. Let us take our candles with us and use them this week in the candlelight memorial march against AIDS. Let us go forth in love. Amen. Blessed be. Let it be so.

LITANY FOR THE AIDS CRISIS

Paul A. Tucker

ONE: For those whose bodies have been invaded by HIV, we call on our God.

ALL: O God of Compassion, hear our prayer.

ONE: For those who have lost friends, lovers, spouses, or family members, that their memory may remain gentle on our minds and that we may pick up the pieces of our lives, we pray to our God.

ALL: O God of Compassion, hear our prayer.

ONE: For those who know the fear of asking, Am I next? and who panic at the sight of rashes, colds, or swollen lymph nodes, we pray to our God.

ALL: O God of Compassion, hear our prayer.

ONE: For the worried well and those who lack the facts; may their minds be opened to information that, looking, they may see and know the truth, we pray to our God.

ALL: O God of Compassion, hear our prayer.

ONE: We lift up to God our world where prejudice is used to divide us; where social systems teach hatred, homophobia, and bigotry. May God bring order to our chaos, we pray to our God.

ALL: O God of Compassion, hear our prayer.

ONE: For those who work tirelessly to find a cure, a vaccine, an insight that our world may have hope, we pray to our God.

ALL: O God of Compassion, hear our prayer.

ONE: For the determination to see this crisis through to the end, we pray to you, our God.

ALL: O God of Compassion, hear our prayer.

ONE: O God, we believe that you have heard our prayer. May the faith of our hearts become the action of our hands that your reconciling and healing love may be made known to all the world, we pray to our God.

ALL: O God of Compassion, hear our prayer.

COMMUNITY MEMORIAL SERVICE

A. Stephen Pieters

Prelude

(*The music at this memorial service should soar, allowing the spirit to soar and feel the height and depth of grief.*)

Call to Worship

ONE: How long, O Lord? How long will we have to wear red and pink ribbons, and teach and practice safer sex?

MANY: Open our eyes, that we may see the truth.

ONE: How long, O Lord? How long must we watch people we love lose breasts or limbs or organs, or waste away with disease?

MANY: Open our ears, that we may hear the truth.

ONE: How long, O Lord? How long must we continue to live with the deaths of people we love? How long must we grieve?

MANY: Open our hearts, that we may feel the truth.

ONE: Help us to grieve, that we may risk loving again.

MANY: We will open our mouths to sing your praise, O God, because you have stayed with us, even in our grief, and will stay with us through it all.

Hymn of Praise

Prayer of Confession

ALL: Loving and Most Amazing God, when we sing your praises, we are reminded of our own faithlessness. We remember the ways we have doubted your presence in the midst of our struggles with HIV/AIDS, cancer, and other life-threatening illnesses. We recall the times we have stopped ourselves from feeling our grief because we felt it wasn't faithful. We confess the times we have cried out in anger at you. We thank you that you can take it and still love us, just the way we are.

Assurance of Pardon

The Gloria

The Reading of the Word

Suggested scripture: John 11:17–27

Choral Anthem

Sermon

Hymn of Response

Offertory

Act of Remembrance

(*At this time, each individual is invited to rise as each is able, state the name of someone who has died, and move to the back of the sanctuary, leaving each chair empty in memory of the one who has died.*)

WORSHIP LEADER: As we contemplate these empty chairs, let us vow to make our lives living and loving memorials to those we have loved who have preceded us in death.

(*As the congregation returns to their seats, there may be singing:*)

A Hymn of Consolation or a Choral Anthem

Affirmation of Faith

Recessional Hymn

Benediction

(*May be read by two readers or responsively.*)

ONE: The Lord said to Abraham,
MANY: Do not be afraid.
ONE: The Lord said to Isaac,
MANY: Do not be afraid.
ONE: Moses said to the people,
MANY: Do not be afraid.
ONE: Joshua said to the people,
MANY: Do not be afraid.
ONE: Boaz said to Ruth,
MANY: Do not be afraid.
ONE: Jonathan said to David,
MANY: Do not be afraid.
ONE: The angel of the Lord said to Joseph,
MANY: Do not be afraid.
ONE: The angel said to Mary,
MANY: Do not be afraid.
ONE: The angel said to the shepherds,
MANY: Do not be afraid.
ONE: The angel said to the women at the tomb,

MANY: Do not be afraid.

ONE: The Lord said to Paul,

MANY: Do not be afraid.

ONE: And Jesus said,

MANY: Do not be afraid; just have faith.

ONE: Let us not be afraid as we go into the world, fully alive in the love of God through Jesus Christ, our Sovereign and Savior.

ALL: Amen.

Postlude

GRAVESIDE SERVICE FOR A GAY MAN WHO HAS DIED YOUNG

Zalmon Sherwood

(*Friends and family gather at the cemetery for burial. The body is in a simple wooden coffin that is placed beside the open grave. Flowers may be placed on the coffin and around the grave.*)

Opening Words

READER: We meet on holy ground,
     for that place is holy where we meet one another.
     Where lives touch, where love moves, where hope stirs,
     there is holy ground.
     How strong our need is for one another.
     Our silent beckoning to our neighbors,
     our invitations to share life and death together,
     our welcome into the lives of those we meet,
     and their welcome into our own.
     We meet on holy ground,
     brought into being as life encounters life,
     as personal histories merge into the communal story,
     as we take on the pride and pain of our companions,
     as our separate selves become community.
     We meet on holy ground.
     Let us pray. Jesus our brother,
     you know the depth of our sorrow.
     You also wept for Lazarus, your dear friend who died.

Bless all who mourn N.'s death.
Let us not hide from this pain in words or busy actions.
Keep us open to the depths of love
and our need for one another.
Let our tears flow as your love flows over us.
As you have blessed us in our loving,
bless us in our parting.
Let our love be bonded forever.

ALL: Amen.

READER: Beneath the canopy of the infinite heavens and in this place of peace, set apart from the world's stress and grief,

ALL: We pray for an understanding of the agelong mystery of death and mystery of life.

READER: Into the friendly earth that has served as a final resting place of innumerable bodies of those who have lived before us,

ALL: We commit the body of our friend, N., his beauty welcome with ready love, his earthly span too brief, his departure so devastating.

READER: Like a shooting star he arrived, flashed across our vision, then was gone.

ALL: We are moved to shock and tears.
We weep, we pray. We are angry.
We accuse fate, but we cannot alter it.
We mourn, we cry until we are numb.
If we feel, it is only loneliness, fear, desolation, and rage.
Others try to comfort us, but they can't feel our loss
or know our sadness.
We know healing will take time.
We know we will smile again, and laugh, and sing.
We know that.
But for now, we are not whole.
We think only how much we miss you, N.,
now that you're gone.

(*Friends and family carefully lift the coffin and lower it into the grave. With a spade, each participant takes turns silently filling the grave with soil. When the grave has been filled, flowers may be strewn across it.*)

READER: The song is done, the western sun sets, the stars repose in the darkened sky.

ALL: Our brother no longer hears the birds, feels the warmth of the sun, ponders the vast expanse of space.

READER: The bell has tolled for him, the candle has been spent, the flower that bloomed so brightly has faded.

ALL: Our brother no longer joins our circle, holds our hand, smiles or cries with us.

READER: How can such a loving heart be shut into the hard ground? Into the darkness he goes, this wise and lovely man.

ALL: Friends and lovers, into the earth with you. Be one with the dull, indiscriminate dust.

READER: His answers quick and keen, his honesty, compassion, love, his sexiness. They are gone, all gone.

ALL: More precious was the light in his eyes than all the stars dancing circles in the night.

READER: Down, down, down into the darkness of the grave. Gently he goes, the beautiful, the tender, the kind.

ALL: Quietly he goes, the intelligent, the witty, the brave. Crowned with lilies and with laurel he goes. But we do not approve. And we are not resigned.

FUNERAL FOR A LESBIAN ACTIVIST: CELEBRATING THE LIFE OF N.

Zalmon Sherwood and *Kittredge Cherry*

The following service takes place in a church with the body present. The coffin is closed and draped with a quilt or other decorative pall that is appropriate for the deceased woman. Guests enter quietly and may place flowers on the coffin. One or more photos may be displayed on the altar, along with important mementos from her life.

Opening Music and Meditation

(*Quiet instrumental or vocal music, suitable for meditation.*)

Opening Words

READER: We have gathered this day to remember, with love, our friend N., who has died. She was a lesbian, lover of women, friend of the oppressed.

ALL: Although our sadness is great, we are thankful that we knew her. N. was a good friend, a dedicated teacher, an active feminist, mother to N., partner of N., and we loved her.

READER: In the midst of life, we are in death. The spirit of our beloved sister dwells in our hearts.

ALL: We have the courage, in love, to carry forward her memory in the lives we lead now.

READER: O Great Goddess, receive from us the person of N. Let the best that was her be renewed in strength in us.

ALL: May we now give to others the love that we no longer can give to her. For the lives we lead are now her honor and her memorial.

READER: She would bless our courage. May we dwell in peace. She would wish it so.

Prayer

READER: Let us pray. Goddess of Kindness, look upon us in our sorrow for this life taken from us. Gather our pain into your peace. Heal our memories, be present in our grieving and overcome all our doubts. Awaken our gratitude for your gifts of love and tenderness. As we are able to receive them, teach us the lessons of life that can be learned in death.

Welcome

Song

(If the deceased had a favorite song or hymn, it could be sung at this time. Otherwise, any music that addresses the woman's life and mission is appropriate.)

Reading

(Read a selection from the writings of the deceased or her favorite poem or essay.)

A Time for Remembering N.

(The officiant invites the people gathered to come forward in turn and briefly share a favorite memory they have of the deceased. The officiant should remain near each speaker to lend support, in case they are overcome by grief, and to ensure that time is honored. This section moves more smoothly if a few speakers are asked in advance to prepare their remarks. The time for remembering generally evokes both laughter and tears; it is the heart of this funeral service.)

Words of Consolation

ALL: We are blessed with the gift of friendship, the bonding of persons in a circle of love, friends who share our sorrows, who bear our pain, who need us as we need them, who weep as we weep, who hold us when words fail, and who give us the freedom to be ourselves.

READER: We give thanks for the life and witness of our sister N., who made our world a better place.

ALL: She believed that equality comes first, peace with justice is the goal, reason is imperative, and love conquers all.

READER: She touched the lives of all she met.

ALL: With wit and wisdom, with zest and zeal, and with dogged determination.

READER: O Great Spirit, grant that she may lie down in peace.

ALL: O Dear One, grant that she may rise up again to life.

READER: May we one day see again her shining face.

ALL: May we one day feel again her warm embrace.

READER: May the peace of the Goddess go in our hearts, merry meet and merry part and merry meet again.

ALL: Blessed be, blessed be, blessed be.

Closing Words

Unto the Goddess's mercy, protection, and love we commit you, N. We cherish the memory of your words, your deeds, and your character. May you dwell in peace and light forever. We shall never forget you as we continue your work toward justice and dignity for all.

Closing Music

(*Joyful, spirited instrumental music is appropriate as guests depart.*)

YOM HASHOAH: DAY OF REMEMBERING THE HOLOCAUST

Steve Carson

Background

The Jewish calendar now includes a day of commemorating the Holocaust, the murder of over six million Jews and millions of others by the Nazis during World War II. This day, called Yom HaShoah, is observed on the twenty-seventh of Nisan, which usually falls on or near the second Sunday after Easter. (A local temple, synagogue, or Jewish community center can supply the dates and inform you of other observances taking place as well.)

Commemorating such an observance can have many meanings for lesbian and gay Christians. We remember the homosexuals who were marked by the Nazis with the pink triangle and who shared in this destruction. As Christians, we acknowledge and confess our connection with these events, which occurred in the heart of Christian Europe. We recognize in our own time the voices of intolerance and hatred that echo throughout history. As people of faith, we commit ourselves to a world of justice, where diversity is welcomed and embraced.

Observing Yom HaShoah can be an opportunity for an interfaith service with people from many traditions participating. It can also be incorporated into the Sunday worship of an individual church. If the service includes Communion, connections to the tradition of the Passover meal may be made. These suggestions and guidelines have proven effective in Yom HaShoah services that have taken place in Boston and San Francisco. They can be freely adapted for local use.

In addition to readings and music that shape the liturgy and inform the sermon, I describe here three liturgical pieces that can be incorporated into a Yom HaShoah commemoration: a statement of context called "We All Wear the Triangle," a liturgy for the "Lighting of the Candle of Remembrance," and "Reciting the Mourners' Kaddish." The lighting of the candle may occur at any point in the service. The Mourners' Kaddish may be part of a general time of prayer or remembrance. In an interfaith service, or if members of the congregation know Hebrew, the Kaddish can be first prayed in Hebrew, and then by everyone in English. Hearing the Hebrew adds meaning for both Jewish and non-Jewish attenders.

Readings

Scripture may be chosen from the Hebrew Bible, which is a sacred text common to both Christians and Jews. Appropriate readings include Lam. 1:1–3 and Isa. 65:17–25. It is effective to have readings spoken in both Hebrew and English. The Twenty-third Psalm can be read responsively as a Call to Worship. Readings can also include contemporary accounts of the Holocaust, such as excerpts from Elie Wiesel's *Night*.

Music

Many hymns have as their basis texts from the Hebrew Bible. These include "O God, Our Help in Ages Past" (St. Anne), "Praise to the Living God" (Leoni), and "The God of Love My Comfort Is" (St.

Columba). The scriptural basis for each hymn often appears at the back of many hymnals. Beginning the service with music for gathering, such as traditional Jewish songs like "Hiney Mah Tov" and "Shalom Chaverim," can create a spirit for the service. Other contemporary songs from the lesbian and gay movement, such as "Singing for Our Lives" by Holly Near, can also be effective. This music is available from Redwood Cultural Work, P.O. Box 10408, Oakland, California 94610.

We All Wear the Triangle

(*May be read by two leaders or responsively.*)

ONE: We are in many ways a culture without memory. The Holocaust, a series of events that occurred just over a generation ago, changed the world forever. Yet by some the Holocaust is forgotten, or seen as irrelevant, or even viewed as something that never happened.

ALL: As people of faith, we refuse to forget. We refuse to participate in the erasing of history. As a community of faith, we decide to remember, as we hear the historical record from Europe a generation ago and reflect upon events in our time. We dare to listen to the voices of the past, even as they echo today.

ONE: In this moment, we are all Jews wearing the yellow Star of David.

ALL: We are all homosexuals wearing the pink triangle.

ONE: We are all political activists wearing the red triangle.

ALL: We are all criminals wearing the green triangle.

ONE: We are all antisocials wearing the black triangle.

ALL: We are all Jehovah's Witnesses wearing the purple triangle.

ONE: We are all emigrants wearing the blue triangle.

ALL: We are all Gypsies wearing the brown triangle.

ONE: We are all undesirable, all expendable by the state.

Lighting the Candle of Remembrance

LEADER: In this moment, the world pauses to remember. We stand together in this sacred moment, made holy by our sense of the past and our vision of the future.

We light this candle to the memory of the six million Jewish people who died martyrs' deaths at the hands of the Nazis and their collaborators; and to the memory of the communities and institutions that were destroyed in an attempt to erase the name and culture of Israel.

We remember the events of fifty years ago, at Dachau, Auschwitz, Buchenwald, Bergen-Belsen, Treblinka, Birkenau, and Sobibór.

We remember the besieged fighters of the ghettos, who rose and kindled the flame of revolt to save the honor of their people.

We remember the righteous Gentiles among the nations who risked their lives to save Jews from persecution and death.

We remember the lesbians and gay men who wore the pink triangle and shared this destruction by the Nazis.

We remember all the minorities, political prisoners, Gypsies, handicapped, and others, who went to their deaths under the tyranny of the Third Reich.

We light this candle to affirm our inseparable connection with the people of Israel and the God of Israel, who is our God, the God of Life.

To God of both memory and hope, we pledge ourselves to be a people of resistance to the powers of death wherever they may appear, to honor the living and the dead, and to make with them our promise: Never again!

Reading

(*A selection from the diary of Anne Frank would be appropriate.*)

Reciting the Mourners' Kaddish

LEADER: The Mourners' Kaddish is a traditional Jewish prayer that is part of the process of grieving and remembering the dead. It is traditionally recited daily by the family and loved ones for the first month following someone's death, and then each year thereafter on the anniversary of that person's death.

On Yom HaShoah, it is appropriate for the congregation to join together in reciting the Kaddish, because for many of those consumed in the Holocaust, there is no one left to pray this prayer.

I invite you to rise as you are able as we pray together this prayer, praying in English after hearing read the traditional Hebrew words.

In recalling our dead of blessed memory, we confront our loss with faith by rising to praise God's name in public assembly, praying that all will soon recognize God's sovereignty over all the world. For when God's sovereignty is felt in all the world, blessing and song fill the world, as well as great consolation.

(*Read the traditional Jewish Kaddish, first in Hebrew, then in English.*)

4

Rites
of Blessing

To bless is to recognize, to affirm, to lift up, to support, to protect, to claim divine approval. People traditionally seek blessings from ordained clergy. Clergy routinely convey blessings upon a variety of objects and persons, but many religious traditions withhold such blessings when dealing with lesbians and gay men. In fact, lesbians and gay men historically have received more curses than blessings from religious authorities.

Lesbians and gay men have had to look beyond ecclesiastical circles for divine approval. They realize that blessings are likely to occur in the most unlikely places: in their service to those who are ill or in need, in their political activity to end discrimination, in the arms of their lovers or friends.

HOME BLESSING

James Lancaster

(Participants gather outside the home—in the yard or hallway if feasible; otherwise, in a central room. Blesser may be the resident(s), an appointed friend, a minister, or a group of people. Although nothing is required, you may use implements like a censor, tray of cedar or sweetgrass, something to sprinkle water, or anything that suggests cleaning.)

RESIDENT(S): Welcome to our home.

BLESSER: We come to N.'s home to bless it and prepare it for their living here. We come to this dwelling mindful of our many brothers and sisters, lesbian and gay, straight, people with AIDS, and others of all races and conditions who have neither shelter nor a secure place to rest their heads and live in private dignity. We are grateful for the blessing of this home. May this blessing ceremony strengthen us all so that we may minister more effectively to those who are homeless.

(All turn to face the front door.)

BLESSER: We, gathered here, spread a protective blanket of peace over and around this dwelling. We surround it with the light of God and envelop it in the soothing darkness of intimacy. We pray that it be kept safe from intruders and all hostilities. May this home be a source of strength for all in this community.

(If the participants are outside, they now enter the home and move into a central area, where the group surrounds the resident(s).)

BLESSER: God of comfort and freedom, of power and dark mystery, scatter your blessings upon this home and fill it with the smoke of your cleansing Spirit. Drive away all spirits of oppressiveness, of violence, of grief, and of all destructive powers that come to its doors or that may have ever existed in this place. Gather together all spirits of tenderness, peace, and life-giving love to guard its corners and keep this hearth. Encircle this home with your robe of mercy and grace, and fill it to the brimming with all good things. In your mercy,

ALL: Hear our prayer.

BLESSER: Holy God, you redeemed the Israelites of old from out of the house of bondage, just as you redeemed the African Americans of our own country from the chains of slavery. Through all time you have brought wanderers safely home. Protect this home and all who sojourn here from the bondage of homophobic violence, from racial hatred, from cruelty and abuse, and from all attacks on these gentle people and those who share their hospitality. In your mercy,

ALL: Hear our prayer.

BLESSER: Grant all who enter here a share in your bounty and cover each person with the soft shelter of your wings. May each visitor leave any grudge, malice, or cruelty at the door, and have such a wondrous time that they forget to collect them when they leave. In your mercy,

ALL: Hear our prayer.

(*Communal prayers may now be offered, as individual participants share the blessings they have for the resident(s). If an implement of fire or water is to be used, prepare it and move from room to room or between different areas in the dwelling. Cense or sprinkle all windows, doors, and openings to the exterior of the dwelling, including crawl spaces into attics or basements, if accessible. Be especially sure to get all the closets. Say the following blessing in the center of each room or area:*)

BLESSER: This room is sacred space, holy to all who live and visit this home. It is sealed with the power of God and guarded by the shining spirits of Ruth and Naomi, and of Jonathan and David, fellow travelers with us who found a home in each other. There is no place for evil here.

(*Alternate line for closet blessings:*)

There is no place for destructive secrets or other evil here.

(*After all areas of the home have been blessed, gather again in a central room.*)

BLESSER: Let us pray: Sweet baby Jesus, you yourself had no place to lay your head. Too often have lesbian and gay people been driven from their homes and communities, and had their family and friends, their identities, and even their lives taken away from them. You know how vital it is to have a place that is free from danger in order to live, rest, and recreate. Create with us in this home a sacred, holy place. Fill it and all who live and play here with comfort, love, and all your tender mercies. Protect the traveling of all who come and all who leave, and bring us all to a safe and secure home. Amen.

ALL: Amen.

BLESSER: Go—and stay—in peace, and serve God.

ALL: Thanks be to God.

ANIMAL BLESSING SERVICE

Kittredge Cherry

Animals are important in the lives of many lesbian and gay people. Cats and dogs often become surrogate children for same-sex couples. The health benefits provided by living with an animal companion are well known, and in several cities gay and lesbian people have helped create unique organizations such as PAWS (Pets Are Wonderful Support) dedicated to enabling people with AIDS to keep their pets.

On a more philosophical level, the discrimination faced by lesbian and gay people is linked to attitudes that devalue animals and the rest of nature. Western thought sets up dualities in which spirit is better than body, male is better than female, human is better than animal, intellectual is better than sexual—and sexuality defines gays and lesbians in this way of thinking. Gays and lesbians, like nature itself, are seen as something that must be controlled. The result is a sterile, exclusive church and a polluted earth. Many lesbians and gay men seek to remedy this situation by healing the spirit-body split in Christianity. For all these reasons, it is appropriate to bless animals in the context of lesbian and gay spirituality.

Animal blessing is rooted in the Middle Ages, when the church blessed the livestock and crops on which the rural community depended. Contemporary animal blessings are often practiced in the Episcopal and Roman Catholic traditions on the Feast of St. Francis of Assisi on October 4 (or the Sunday nearest). The most famous and elaborate of these services is the annual Earth Mass at the Cathedral of St. John the Divine in New York City, featuring the music of the Paul Winter Consort. An elephant, camel, falcon, python, blue-green algae, and other creatures process into St. John's, the world's largest Gothic cathedral, to receive a blessing, while thousands of other creatures sit in the pews with their human companions. Dogs bark along with the choir, and people receive Communion with cats in their arms. After the service, priests spend the afternoon blessing individual animals, while around them a fair takes place featuring animal adoptions, a petting zoo, vegetarian food, booths with representatives of environmental concerns and animal rights groups, and an animal/owner look-alike contest with prizes. (Lesbian/gay celebrations have added such categories as "Best Costume," "Best Trick," "Most Butch" and "Most Femme"—all referring to the animal, not the owner.) Any or all of this can serve as a model for other communities that want to create an animal blessing ceremony.

The following service is designed for the Feast of St. Francis, but it could be conducted on Earth Day (April 22) or another appropriate day chosen by a worshiping community. It incorporates a canticle by St.

Francis (1182[?]–1226), who is famous for his love of animals, his ability to see beauty in everyday life, and his passion for peace and the poor. Like many lesbian and gay people, he never married and was estranged from his family. He called all creatures brother or sister because he knew their source was the same as his. Congregants should be encouraged to bring their animals to the service.

Call to Worship

(*Based on "The Canticle to Brother Sun" by St. Francis of Assisi, read responsively.*)

Opening Hymn

"Morning Has Broken"

Opening Prayer

LEADER: Life-giving Spirit,
　　You provide all things, and all things belong to you. Thank you for the earth whose many breasts nourish the plants, the fish, the birds, the animals, and us. We see your holy image in the diversity of all life forms. Humankind, too, reflects your glory in the wondrous variety of race, gender, physical ability, and sexual orientation that you have created in us. Grant that, following the example of St. Francis, we may for love of you delight in all your creatures and live in harmony with them, to the honor of your name. Amen.

Welcome and Announcements

Greeting of Peace

Choir Anthem

"Blue Green Hills of Earth," music and words by Kim Oler
(*The copyright for this anthem is 1986 by Hendon Music, Inc., a Boosey & Hawkes company.*)

Scripture Readings

Appropriate Bible readings include Gen. 1:20–31 (creation of the earth); Gen. 9:8–11 (God's covenant with Noah and all creatures); Ps. 148:7–10 (a call for sea monsters and other creatures to praise God); Eccl. 3:19–21 (the shared fate of humankind and animals); Isa. 11:6–8 (vision of the wolf dwelling with the lamb); Matt. 6:25–33 (God's care for birds and lilies); Mark 1:12 (Jesus with the wild beasts); and Mark 16:14–15 (Jesus proclaims the gospel is for "all creatures"). A variety of other sources, especially Native American writings, also offer readings on humanity and nature.

Sermon

(*Appropriate sermon themes address the relationship between humanity and creation.*)

Prayer Hymn

"Peace Prayer" by John Foley (*based on a prayer of St. Francis, available from North American Liturgy Resources, Phoenix, Arizona*)

Community Prayer

LEADER: You are invited to join hands with those sitting near you while we pray as a symbol of the connections that join all of creation.

God, our Creator and Sustainer,

May we remember that the earth does not belong to us, but we belong to the earth. We are dust, and to dust we shall return. In the words of Isaiah, "Surely, the people is grass."

May we remember that humanity is but one small, fragile strand in the interdependent web of life.

May we remember that we human beings are not the only ones created to look at flowers, to taste cool water, to listen to the wind, and to feel the earth beneath our feet.

May we remember that what befalls the earth befalls all who live on her lovely shores.

May we never forget that to harm the earth is to scorn the Creator.

We pray for the animals who are our companions.

We pray for the wildlife displaced as we develop land for human use.

We pray for the animals who work for us, including the seeing-eye dog, the carriage horse, and the laboratory rat.

We pray for animals who are bought and sold, animals who live in cages, and animals who live free.

We pray for animals indigenous to this particular place, including [*Name a few species*].

We pray for the animals who have made our lives possible by becoming food and clothing for us.

We pray for endangered species, including the giant panda and the California condor, and we remember the dinosaurs, passenger pigeons, and other extinct species.

We pray for all human beings who have felt degraded by being compared to animals.

God, we know that you hear all our prayers, those spoken and those that we hold silently in our hearts. We claim your loving presence with us now as we conclude with the prayer that Jesus taught us.

(*Congregation then prays aloud what is traditionally called the Lord's Prayer.*)

The Offering of Tithes and Gifts

Offertory Choir Anthem

"From a Distance" by Julie Gold

Communion Hymn

"All Creatures of the Earth and Sky"

Celebration and Sharing of Communion

(*Animals may accompany worshipers as they receive Communion.*)

The Blessing of the Animals

(*A few representative animals come forward and the worship leaders bless them, saying something like "God bless the universe, and all creatures in it, great and small." Personalized blessings should be offered after the service. Blessing may be done by laying on of hands, sprinkling of holy water, or a simple prayer over the creature. Individual blessings should be improvised; a typical prayer might be this: "Loving God, thank you for our sister, Ambush the cat. She praises you through her graceful movement, sleek softness, playful spirit, and gentle purr. Bless her that she may receive many years of health and happiness. In Christ's name we pray, Amen."*)

Closing Prayer

LEADER: Yahweh, El Shaddai, Energy Sacred,
Every part of this earth is holy to you: Every sparrow, every pine needle, every squirrel, every whale. We praise you for all creation, and we pray that we may live in balance with all animal and plant life, safeguarding them for posterity. The wind that gave our grandparents their first breath will also give breath to our grandchildren. May

it always be pure, sweetened by fragrant flowers and by the knowledge of your divine presence. In Christ's name we pray. Amen.

Closing Hymn

When Israel Camped in Sinai
(*Tune: Webb, "Stand Up, Stand Up for Jesus"; lyrics by Laurence G. Bernier, 1974, copyright UFMCC.*)

> When Israel camped in Sinai, God spoke and Moses heard,
> This message tell the people, and give them this my word,
> From Egypt I was with you; I bore you on my wing,
> The whole of your great nation from slav'ry I did bring.
>
> Just as a mother eagle who helps her young to fly,
> I am a mother to you; your needs I will supply,
> And you are as my children, my own who hear my voice,
> I am a mother to you, the people of my choice.
>
> If God is like an eagle who helps her young to fly,
> And God is also father, then what of you and I?
> We have no fear of labels; we have no fear of roles,
> God blends them and transcends them; we seek the self-same goal.
>
> Our God is not a woman; our God is not a man.
> Our God is both and neither, our God is I who am.
> From all the roles that bind us, our God has set us free.
> What freedom does God give us? The freedom just to be.

RITE OF BLESSING:
FOR THE DEDICATION OF NEW HYMNALS

Nancy Wilson

Many Metropolitan Community Churches, reconciling churches, and lesbian/gay-identified congregations in other denominations are experimenting with new inclusive-language hymnals. These hymnals also include lesbian/gay-oriented hymns, feminist hymns, and hymns of racial/ethnic diversity and musical diversity.

The significance of the new hymnals is more than just to "modernize." They express the new theology, ethic, and "spiritual culture" that is emerging through the lesbian/gay movement.

If a new hymnal is replacing an older, more traditional version, involve congregational leaders and members by inviting their input in the selection of a hymnal, or of hymns (if you are creating your own). Box up the old hymnals and make arrangements to send them to a church that wants and needs them.

(As people arrive for worship, have the new hymnals in the pews or on the chairs. The rite of blessing may be done before the processional hymn. Or, more dramatically, have the old and new hymnals side by side in the seats. Use the old hymnal for the processional hymn—then, as the dedication begins, collect them or have people bring them forward and place them in a box for shipping.)

Opening Words

(Begin with a very brief summary of the process of the creation or selection of the new hymnal. Acknowledge donations of time, talent, and money. Briefly mention the new features and benefits of this hymnal. Then talk about the old hymnals, remembering anyone special who may have donated them.)

Blessing of the Old Hymnals

LEADER: Almighty God, we thank you for the blessing these hymnals have been. We have worshiped with them Sunday after Sunday, at funerals and holy unions, on joyful and solemn occasions. We gratefully acknowledge *those* [*You may name them here*] who made it possible for us to have these hymnals. As they travel to a new church home, may they once again provide joy and praise in worshiping you. In Christ's name we pray. Amen.

Scripture

Suggested readings: 1 Cor. 14:26, Eph. 5:19, or Col. 3:16.

Blessing of the New Hymnals

(Invite the creators or the hymnal selection committee to come forward, each holding a hymnal.)

LEADER: Brothers and sisters, it is time for our congregation to "sing a new song." Please hold a new hymnal in your hands this morning and pray this prayer with me:

ALL: Spirit of the Living God, fall afresh on us today. Help us to sing the songs of Zion, to raise our hearts and voices in love and praise to you. May this new hymnal, a labor of love, be a blessing for many years to come in our church. We bless these new hymnals now in the name of God our Creator, Jesus Christ our Savior, and the Holy Spirit. Amen.

Hymn

Sing a selection from the new hymnal.

MOTORCYCLE BLESSING: THE BLESSING OF THE BIKES

Steve Carson

Bike clubs, like the leather community with which they are associated, represent wide-ranging and diverse interests, expressions, and walks of life. The leather community has for many years been an established and influential segment of the larger gay and lesbian community. Bike clubs and leather bars provide a sexual and social network that includes such features as entertainment events, beer blasts, and funding for charities and community service organizations.

In San Francisco, there is an annual tradition known as the Blessing of the Bikes. Begun by Harry Harkness in the early 1980s, this event happens every summer at the Eagle, a leather bar.

There has long been in the history of the church a tradition of annual blessings that provide a special interaction between the church and the needs of the community. In medieval times, the church would offer blessings on crops and animals. In many seafaring communities, sailors and fishers to this day participate in the church's blessing of the ships. While these blessings seem quaint to modern culture, they often have real meaning to people whose livelihood may depend upon the forces of nature.

This liturgy is an opportunity to bridge the gap between the sacred and the secular. It is an opportunity to hold an ecumenical or interfaith event. Bikers reflect the larger gay and lesbian community in that they come from all backgrounds, churched and unchurched. What they share is enthusiasm and pride in their identity as part of this community.

During the service, keep things simple, clear, and to the point. Your own words are best. A spirit of openness and good humor will be appreciated. Possible themes for remarks and prayers include freedom, the open road, safety and protection, and community.

This can be a peculiarly moving event. Bikers form a genuine community in which people know and respect each other. Bikers are very serious about their motorcycles and feel a strong bond and relationship to them. This group is ignored, misunderstood, or condemned by many religious bodies, yet I have found it to be a deeply spiritual community. Worship leaders will be genuinely welcomed and appreciated, and may find among the leather and the varooms of motorcycles a spiritual event more real than many they have been in before.

(Robes or vestments for worship leaders can provide a visible sense of order and dignity. A leather stole would be appropriate. Bikers should line up with their bikes on the street. Arrangements might be made to have the block closed off to regular traffic. A simple podium with a microphone can be set up on the sidewalk facing the bikes. After some time for socializing, someone should ask participants to take their places.)

Welcome/Introduction of Those Leading the Service

Statement of Gathering

LEADER: For many years and in many traditions, people have gathered to ask God's blessing at particular times for particular purposes. People of the land gather to ask God's blessing upon the planting of crops and the raising of animals. People of the sea gather to this day for the blessing of the ships. People throughout time have recognized the powers of the forces of nature and the importance of coming together with common intent to pray for safety and well-being. In that tradition we gather today for the Blessing of the Bikes. We come together to celebrate this community, the sharing of our lives together. We believe God is present in all places and that God finds expression in the rich diversity of human community. We come together to celebrate the freedom we find as we travel the open road. We come together to ask God's guidance and protection this day and in the days to come.

Reading

A selection from Walt Whitman's "Song of the Open Road"

Community Prayer

LEADER: Spirit of Life, Spirit of the Open Road, in whom we live and move and have our being, be here among us now as we gather in this place. We know you are present, within us and among us. We know you travel with us on the open road, our companion and guide on life's journey. We give thanks for the life of each person here today. We give thanks for the gift of this community in which we find companions on the road. We remember the company of those who are no longer with us, yet who are present in spirit and continue to live in our hearts and in our lives. They too travel with us on the open road. We thank you for the freedom and the joy of our lives together. We come together now to ask your blessings this day and for the year to come. Lead us, guide us, protect us this day and every day. In your many names we pray. Amen.

Personal Prayers and Blessing of the Bikes

(*The worship leaders move from person to person, taking a moment to offer each a prayer of blessing. Taking cues from the person and respecting his or her boundaries, it is often appropriate, in the tradition of laying on of hands as a sign of blessing, to touch both the person and the bike. The prayer should be simple. Ask the person's name, and ask if the bike has a name. The prayer that follows is a model.*)

LEADER: God, we give you thanks this day for the gift of life, which comes from you. We thank you for the spirit of freedom we experience on the open road. We pray now for safety, that N. and N.'s bike may be partners on the road, alert and careful as they travel together. We thank you for this community where we find friendship and love. We thank you for all the places we have been in this life and ask that you bless us now as we set out on the journey that lies before us. Be with us, protect us, guide us. In your many names we pray. Amen.

(*Worship leaders may give each person a token, such as a small rainbow pin or similar item to mark the occasion.*)

Benediction

LEADER: Let us go out into the world in peace, trusting in the protection and guidance of God's spirit, with us wherever we go. Amen. Ladies and gentlemen, you may start your engines.

5

Seasonal
and Holiday Rites

Major holidays such as Thanksgiving and Christmas often pose a dilemma for lesbians and gay men. During the holiday season, people want to be among their loved ones. Some lesbians and gay men may long to celebrate the holidays with their immediate family, their parents and siblings, but for various reasons, they may not feel welcome in such settings. Much of the sense of wonder and awe people traditionally associate with holidays can be lost when people are separated from loved ones or when minorities' lives are marked by discrimination, exploitation, and abuse.

The following rites focus on holidays and seasons of the Christian liturgical year. Symbols and images used address specific lesbian and gay concerns during these periods of spiritual observance.

THANKSGIVING RITE

Zalmon Sherwood

Thanksgiving Day is a holiday on which to pause, to take stock of the blessings in our lives, and to share a portion of our bounty with those who are alone and in need of hospitality and care. It is an appropriate time for friends to gather for a meal and to commit ourselves to creating a world where hungry children are fed, the homeless are provided with shelter, and those who suffer oppression are upheld and respected.

Thanksgiving Day ought not to be a day for thanking God for affluence while others go hungry; nor should it be a time to claim God's special blessing on any nation. As a minority religious group, the Pilgrims knew only too well the problems that occur when the interests of God and nation are identified by a dominant religious group. Lesbians and gay men are a pilgrim people in our own right as we search for places where we can express our affection without fear of persecution.

As a way of giving voice to our highest ideals, the following rite may be offered sometime during the Thanksgiving Day celebration. Weather permitting, the community might gather in a yard or a field as a way of paying homage to the earth and its harvest. The rite begins with a prayer expressive of Native American spirituality.

(*A leader invites the gathering to face north and, with arms outstretched, proclaims the prayer, allowing a brief pause before inviting the group to turn and face a new direction. The prayer closes with all facing north again, with arms either outstretched or down at sides.*)

READER 1: We greet you, Spirit of the North. You are the cold, biting wind that blows across our land, that strips the earth of all that is dead and decayed, that robs us of the false securities, so easily blown away. Teach us to place our feet securely on the earth and to see things as they really are, that the coming of your Spirit may find us standing firm in integrity. It is your Spirit whose winds bring the snows of winter, with their fury and their solitude. It is your Spirit who blankets the earth for sleep. Teach us, Spirit of the North, in the solitude of winter, to wait in darkness with the sleeping earth, believing that we, like the earth, already hold within ourselves the seeds of new life.

(*All turn toward the east.*)

READER 2: We greet you, O Spirit of the East. You usher in the dawn on your breeze; you stretch forth your fingers and paint our skies. Awaken in us with each day, new hopes, new dreams of colors, love and joys never before imagined. Fill our bodies with your breath; invigorate us. Carry us to the farthest mountains and beyond. Inspire us that we might reach out to you boldly to grasp the miracles that are given birth with each new dawn.

(*All turn toward the south.*)

READER 3: We greet you, Spirit of the South. You bring the winds of summer and breathe on us the warmth of the sun to soothe and heal our bodies and our spirits. You thaw and soften the coldness of our world; you nudge the seedlings to break through the soil to light. Quicken us, draw us by the urgings of your warm breath to break through the soil of our own barrenness and fear. Drive our roots deep into the earth and stretch our branches full out into the sky. Teach us to hold sacred the memory of the spring rains that we might have the strength to withstand the heat of the day and not become parched and narrow in our love. Lead us to accept fatigue with resignation, knowing that life is not to be rushed, that there is no flower of the field that grows from seed to blossom in a single day.

(*All turn toward the west.*)

READER 4: We greet you, Spirit of the West. You cool our hot and tired bodies, refresh and bring laughter to our hearts. It is you who usher in the setting sun. It is by your power that the sun hangs suspended for endless moments before you catch it with your breath and carry it off into the night. Guide our steps at the end of the day; keep us safe from evil. Fill us with your peace as you enfold us with your great mystery, that we might rest securely in your arms until morning calls us forth again.

(*All turn toward the north.*)

READER 5: We greet you, Great Spirit of the Earth. It was from you we came as from a Mother; you nourish us still and give us shelter. Teach us to walk softly on your lands, to use with care your gifts, to love with tenderness all our brothers and sisters who have been born of your goodness. And when the day comes that you call us back to yourself, help us to return as a friend, to find ourselves embraced, encircled, enfolded in your arms.

(*The community now gathers in a circle for the following litany.*)

READER: On this Thanksgiving Day, let us give thanks for our Mother Earth, for the fragile beauty of nature, for the gift of friendship.

ALL: Blessed are those who stand for truth when all the systems that surround us would urge us to abandon it or compromise.

(*Names of individuals may be called out after each blessing.*)

READER: Blessed are those who wear compassion like a garment, those who have learned to find themselves by losing themselves in another's sorrow.

ALL: Blessed are those who are hungry for goodness, who thirst for truth and righteousness.

READER: Blessed are those whose hearts are free and simple, those who have smashed all false images and are seeking honestly for the truth.

ALL: Blessed are the creators of peace, those who build roads that unite rather than walls that divide, those who bless the world with the healing power of their presence.

READER: Blessed are those whose love has been tried, like gold, in the furnace and found to be precious, genuine, and lasting; blessed are those who have lived their belief out loud, no matter what the cost or pain. On this Thanksgiving Day, let us remember with gratitude and humility that we alone are not responsible for whatever bounty is in our lives.

ALL: We confess that some of our bounty has come at the expense of others, including Native Americans, slaves, migrant workers, and hosts of others.

READER: Some of us look like the people who lived here long ago, so close to this land that their arrival is not recorded. With them we are pilgrims in this land.

ALL: Some of us look like the Spanish, who came in tall ships. They took the land from the Indians and thought it was theirs. With them we are pilgrims in this land.

READER: Some of us look like the English, who also came in tall ships. They took the land from the Indians and the Spanish and thought it was theirs. With them we are pilgrims in this land.

ALL: Some of us look like Africans, who also came in tall ships. They did not choose to come, and they had no land and no freedom. With them we are pilgrims in this land.

READER: Some of us look like Asians, who came in tall ships across the other ocean. They came looking for work and freedom, but many found discrimination and injustice. With them we are pilgrims in this land.

ALL: We are all different. No two of us look or act exactly alike. Together, we are pilgrims in this land.

READER: Gay men and lesbians come in every color. For most of history, we were isolated, alone, attacked. With the pink triangle, we remember that we are pilgrims on this earth.

ALL: Every day and everywhere, there have been pilgrims like us: independent, inventive, caring, and tough. Each of us is unique. All of us together are strong, pilgrims in this land.

READER: With the rainbow we celebrate the vibrance and diversity of lesbian and gay pilgrims. We're everywhere. Every day. And we are forever pilgrims in this land.

ALL: Blessed be, blessed be. We've always been here. We always will be. Pilgrims in this land.

READER: As gay and lesbian pilgrims, we believe it is a matter of faith to stand up for those who cannot stand up for themselves. We believe in recognizing equally and loving all members of the human family, whatever their race, creed, color, gender, sexual orientation, or physical or mental capacity. We believe the earth, its creatures, and the universe are good, beautiful, and sacred parts of creation that must be protected and cared for. We believe that we are born to accept responsibility, to take a stand on vital issues, and to work to secure freedom, justice, and love for all persons.

ALL: We believe it is the divine power within us that gives us courage and stamina to face the truth and to live it, even to die for it. Let us go forth, continuing this celebration in the knowledge that we are pilgrims, that hope for a new world is in our hearts, that the struggle for justice is our calling. Let us greet each other with open arms, with heads held high. Grab hold of the future and change the world as pilgrims in this land.

(Participants may greet each other with an embrace, a kiss, or a gentle touch. The celebration continues with a meal and the opportunity for conversation.)

RITE FOR ADVENT

Chris R. Glaser

(The lines in the liturgical elements may be read antiphonally or responsively.)

Call to Worship

ONE: How long, dear God, how long?
MANY: Our longing cries to thee.

ONE: Come out of your distant closet,
MANY: Our yearning beckons thee.
ONE: Reveal thyself to us in this age,
MANY: Make known thy love for us.

Hymn

(*Tune: Veni Emmanuel, "O Come, O Come, Emmanuel"; adapted from anonymous, translation by John Mason Neale, adapted lyrics copyright © 1994 by Chris R. Glaser. In the following hymn, italicized syllables are to be held two notes, and syllables in boldface are to be held three notes.*)

O come, O come, **Emman**uel,
and ransom captive **Is**rael
that mourns in lonely *exile* here
until the Child of **God** appear.
Rejoice, rejoice, **Emman**uel
shall come to thee, O **Is**rael.

You shaped us in our **mo**ther's wombs,
Those *for* whom the *world* had no room;
You formed our inward *sighs* and dreams,
That we may find all **that** love means.
Rejoice, rejoice, for **Is**rael
gives birth to our **Emman**uel.

We gather now in **hope** and prayer—
Your *bless*ing will **meet** us there—
You will never leave us alone,
Your steadfast love's eternally enthroned.
Rejoice, rejoice, O **Is**rael,
God will come: **Emman**uel.

Prayer

ONE: In the fertile darkness of soil,
    the green of life bursts out of its shell;
    in the fertilized darkness of womb,
    the flesh of life builds cell upon cell.
MANY: Those born in darkness
    have seen life.

ONE: The closet may be a fertile place:
   creativity bursts out of a lonely hell,
   and from a closet fertilized with hope,
   the spirit leaps from a monastic cell.
MANY: Those born in darkness
   have seen life.
ONE: Out of dark soil sprouts new life,
   from dark wombs springs embodied hope.
   Both stretch for the illumination
   of the cosmic kaleidoscope.
MANY: Those born in darkness
   have seen life.
ONE: Dear God,
MANY: we seek your Word embodied
   in life rooted in fertile darkness.
   In life stretching for illumination,
   we await your transforming Word.

Hymn

(*Tune: Picardy, "Let All Mortal Flesh Keep Silence"; adapted from the Liturgy of St. James, translated by Gerard Moultrie, © Chris R. Glaser.*)

Let all mortal flesh show reverence,
And in awe and wondrous delight
Ponder One born from among us
To inspire and to invite
Reconciliation: Christ, God's Word,
Spoken to redeem, reunite.

Child of God, yet born of Mary,
That God's children all may be
One in faith and in baptism,
One in hope and charity;
One in Christ's blood and body
Offered in diversity.

Alleluia! God comes among us,
Blessing us with earthly hands,
Loving us in earthly pleasures,

Leading us to take our stands
For healing love in our broken world,
For sweet justice in our lands.

Scriptures

(*All Advent scriptures are appropriate.*)

Reflections

(*Reflections may be inward and silent, or spoken, sung, acted out, or danced.*)

Prayers of the People

Response: By your Word, we pray.

Hymn

(*Tune: Hyfrydol, "Come, Thou Long-expected Jesus"; adapted from Charles Wesley, adapted lyrics copyright © 1994 by Chris R. Glaser.*)

Come, thou long-expected Jesus,
Born to set thy people free;
From our fears and bonds release us,
Let us find our rest in thee.
Our own strength and consolation,
Hope of all the earth thou art;
Dear desire of every station,
Joy of every loving heart.

Born thy people to deliver,
Born to hallow body-soul,
Born to open up our closets
Born to lead, not control.
Keep us from weak resignation
To the ills that we deplore:
Guide us in thy common purpose,
To our home, become the door.

Benediction

LEADER: Now may the advent of God in our world
give us pause,
may it give us pleasure,

may it give us peace,
now and forevermore. Amen.

RITE FOR LENT

Chris R. Glaser

(*The lines in the liturgical elements of this rite may be read antiphonally or responsively.*)

Prayer

ONE: Lead us not into temptation,
MANY: but deliver us from evil.
ONE: Deliver us from merely seeking acceptance, O God:
MANY: lead us to live the word that transforms our world.
ONE: Lead us not into temptation,
MANY: but deliver us from evil.
ONE: Keep us from putting you to the test, O God:
MANY: lead us to trust in you and in our own worth.
ONE: Lead us not into temptation,
MANY: but deliver us from evil.
ONE: Free us from false choices, O God:
MANY: lead us into the integrity of body and spirit.
ONE: Lead us not into temptation,
MANY: but deliver us from evil.
    For thine is the commonwealth,
    and the power, and the glory
    now and forever. Amen.

Hymn

(*Tune, St. Flavian, "Lord, Who Throughout These Forty Days"; adapted from Claudia F. Hernaman, adapted lyrics copyright © 1994 by Chris R. Glaser.*)

    Christ, who throughout these forty days
    For us did fast and pray,
    Teach us with thee to find our way
    And close by thee to stay.

As thou with tempters did contend
And did the victory win,
O give us strength to strive with those
Who name our love a sin.

And through our days of wilderness
And by our Passion call
The church to penitence and awe
That God's love is for all.

God, send thine angels to our care,
Freed from our suffering past,
So Easters of unending joy
We may receive at last!

Scriptures

(*All Lenten scriptures are appropriate.*)

Reflections

(*Reflections may be inward and silent, or spoken, sung, acted out, or danced.*)

A Prayer to Jesus

ONE: Jesus,
  our fast has been imposed by others,
  our wilderness sojourn their choice more than ours.
MANY: Our fast from the sacraments,
  our fast from ordination:
  our only choice was honesty.
ONE: With the scapegoat of the ancient Hebrews,
  sexual sins of generations
  have been heaped upon our backs,
  and we have been sent away,
  excommunicated, into the wilderness to die.
MANY: Yet we choose life,
  even in our deprivation.
ONE: Jesus, lead us to discern our call
  parallel to your own:
  rebelling against the boundaries,

questioning the self-righteous authorities,
breaking the Sabbath law
to bring healing.
MANY: Jesus,
lead us from the temptations you also faced
of self-preservation,
of proving our origin,
of coercion over persuasion.
ONE: Jesus,
in your temptation you taught us
our survival,
our authority,
our power
do not lie there.
MANY: Jesus,
by your ministry
lead us to give of ourselves so others may live,
grant us the courage to speak from our experience,
and grace us with the power only of love.
ONE: Jesus,
help us understand that giving of ourselves
means not only feeding the multitudes,
MANY: but also overturning tables in the Temple;
ONE: that speaking of our experience
means not only a comforting mountaintop sermon,
MANY: but also rebuking religious and political authorities;
ONE: and that love does not always wear a happy face,
MANY: but may express anger, may grieve, may yearn,
ONE: as you did over God's house of prayer for all peoples,
as you did over Jerusalem's killing of prophets,
as you did from your cross.
Lead us from our temptations, Jesus.
MANY: Deliver us from the evils of our day.
Because the commonwealth that means life,
the glory in which we share,
and the power of love we enjoy
belong to the God whom you serve.
Amen.

REDISCOVERING GOD AS FATHER

Louis F. Kavar

This rite is especially appropriate for Father's Day, although it can be celebrated at any time.

(The congregation gathers, sitting in a circle around a table covered with items conveying images of fatherhood. These may include a pipe, a warm sweater, or a photo of a father and child. Be sure that enough space remains in the middle of the circle for participants to do the readings.)

Hymn of Gathering

"Peace Is Flowing Like a River" or another song of peace

Opening Prayer

LEADER: Father of all people,
  we gather this day in peace—
  peace that comes from you;
  peace that fills our being;
  peace that we share with each other;
  peace that is our hope for the world.
   In this peace,
  empower us to experience you as a loving and nurturing Father,
  a Father who is present to support us;
  a Father who shares joy with us;
  a Father who delights in us.
   Help us to reclaim the fatherly dimension of divine life in a way
  that is not exploitive;
  that is not exclusive;
  that calls us to live in integrity.
   Enable us to remember that your love is given to us
  in more ways than we can imagine:
  as Father and as Mother;
  as Creator and as Sustainer;
  as the Foundation and Completion of our being,
  today and every day. Amen.

Contemporary Reading

Read the closing scene from Arthur Miller's *Death of a Salesman.*

Moments of Silent Reflection

Scriptural Reading

Read the parable of the loving father from Luke 15:11–32.

Shared Reflections

(*The worship leader shares a few observations about the differences between the fathers portrayed in* Death of a Salesman *and the parable of the loving father. The leader then asks members of the congregation to share how these differences are related to their experience of God as Father. Has the image of God as Father been more like that portrayed in* Death of a Salesman *or like the parable of the loving father? What will it take to experience God as portrayed in the parable rather than the kind of father depicted in* Death of a Salesman *? How has your relationship with your own father shaped your perception of the experience of God as Father? And as a gay man, in what ways has the image of God as Father been related to relationships with other men?*)

Prayer of Reconciliation

LEADER: God, our Father, we have been taught that you are
    a God of power and of might;
    a God of vengeance;
    a God of just punishment;
    a God who remembers all our sins;
    a God who judges.
Because of what we have been taught,
it has been difficult to believe that you are the God
who is love, compassion, and tenderness.
    Be with us now as a Loving Father.
Recognize our anger, which has resulted from having been
prevented from knowing you as a good Father
who has our interest at heart,
who supports and nurtures us,
who provides us with the very best of all that is possible.
Reveal yourself to us as a Father
who attentively listens,
who delights in his children,
who supports us with warmth and strength.
    Help us grow beyond the deformative ways you have been
shown to us as a Father to find that you are a sure hope
and a model for us as we

claim our masculinity,
intimately explore our love and sexuality,
relate to other men,
share with our own fathers,
and care for our children.
    Let us know that you patiently wait for us to return to your
home, as did the loving father of the prodigal son.
And we await all the ways you return to our lives,
    today and every day. Amen.

Act of Reconciliation

(*The congregation is asked to share a sign of affirmation with each other,
recognizing the bond of the Loving Father among them.*)

Closing Song

Sending Forth

LEADER: Go forth this day,
    having been affirmed, loved, and reconciled to the One
who is our Father.
Know his gentle compassion in your life now and always.
Amen.

MAUNDY THURSDAY
SERVICE OF FOOT WASHING

Troy D. Perry

Foot washing on Maundy Thursday is a tradition that began with Jesus,
who commanded his disciples to follow his example of washing feet as
part of the Last Supper. The Roman Catholic Church and other mainline denominations observe some form of foot washing on Maundy
Thursday, a holy day that marks Jesus' sharing bread and wine with his
disciples prior to his betrayal and crucifixion. A variety of Protestant
denominations celebrate this rite whenever Communion is served.
They include the Free Will Baptist Church, the Church of God in Christ,
the Pentecostal Holiness Church, and the denomination in which I was
raised, the Church of God. The following service follows the basic
format I used for foot washing in the earliest years of the Universal
Fellowship of Metropolitan Community Churches.
    Materials needed for foot washing include a large towel and a

washbasin filled with water. Arrange a dozen chairs in two rows facing each other. Pairs seated across from each other will take turns washing each other's feet. One person begins by gently holding one of the partner's feet over the basin, sprinkling it with water, and then drying it. The person doing the washing may say a brief prayer such as, "God, as I wash the feet of this *sister/brother,* let me remember that I am always your servant and a servant to the world."

Opening Prayer

Song

"Lord of the Dance"

Scripture Reading

Matthew 26:17–19, 26–30

Reading

The Hebrew children knew slavery. From the time when Joseph had been governor of Egypt to the Exodus, they spent four hundred thirty years as slaves, told that they had no history and no freedom. They were told that they were destined to be used as their oppressors saw fit. With no hope, only fear, they waited from day to day for death to bring their deliverance.

But one day the unbelievable happened! God spoke, someone listened, and the Hebrew children left Egypt and slavery. For hundreds of years the children of Israel remembered their deliverance from slavery by celebrating Passover. It was at such a celebration that Jesus used the story of the Exodus to remind us that we are created free to become servants to one another.

We who are members of the lesbian and gay community know about slavery. We who are part of the faith community also know about deliverance! On October 6, 1968, Metropolitan Community Church was founded in Los Angeles, California, as the first openly lesbian and gay church in the world. Since then, lesbians and gay men have gathered to form their own faith communities in virtually every denomination and religion.

Communion serves as our act of remembrance, our meal of deliverance by which we are set free.

Act of Communion

Song

I'm Not Afraid Anymore
(*Text and music by Michael Mank, copyright 1972 by UFMCC.*)

The Teacher came to earth, to show the way of life;
This peace to bring from heav'n above that all might walk in light.
One time my soul was grieved, Grace was denied to me.
But then Christ's message of love I heard, now I have been set free.
Chorus:
I'm not afraid anymore!
I'm not afraid anymore!
God's message is for all the world,
salvation is for everyone,
what's bound on earth is bound in heav'n.
Praise to God! I'm not afraid anymore!

My friend, do you now feel God has denied you here,
With burdens of this life you lead bound up in guilt and fear?
The Savior now has said, "Come unto me and rest."
Accept this gift of love, my friend, with peace you shall be blessed.
(*Repeat chorus.*)
That Jesus did not come this love with all to share,
I listened to these words of those who really did not care.
But now I am convinced God has prepared the way
For all who trust in Jesus' word believing they shall say,
(*Repeat chorus.*)

Scripture Reading

John 13:2a, 4–6

Reading

Jesus shocked the apostles after the Passover meal by insisting on washing their feet. They could not comprehend why Jesus would want to perform the act of a servant.

We know that Jesus was teaching the apostles, as well as us, a divine truth—with freedom comes responsibility. For to whom much is given, of them much is required.

As freed people of the lesbian and gay community, we must remember that not all members of our community have been delivered from Egypt. Many in our community still suffer from oppression sickness. The act of foot washing reminds us again that we, members of this faith community, are freed servants. We are no longer slaves, but servants to each other.

We wash each other's feet on this Maundy Thursday. We then take this act out into the community. We continue to wash feet when we involve ourselves in caring for those with AIDS, breast cancer, or any life-threatening illness. Other forms of foot washing include housing the homeless, feeding the hungry, clothing the naked, helping to end sexism, racism, and homophobia, and letting peace start with us.

As we wash each other's feet as Jesus did for the apostles, let us remember, we are free!

Act of Washing Feet

Closing Hymn

"It Is Well with My Soul"

Benediction

6

Covenant Rites
for Couples

The word *covenant* refers to a solemn pact or agreement between persons who commit themselves to each other. In the case of lesbian and gay couples, they commit to honor, respect, support, and love each other. Such covenants are intended to be exclusive and permanent, the basis of creating a new family model that not only will have the stability necessary to rear children (if the couple wishes to do so) but also will sustain the partners to the end of their lives. Christian rites of blessing for same-sex couples have been found as far back as the ninth century, predating the church's heterosexual marriage rites by three hundred years.

Debate continues in the lesbian and gay community about whether such ceremonies are "hetero-imitative," and therefore oppressive for same-sex couples, or one of the most radically liberating acts a same-sex couple can undertake. Even agreement about the appropriate name for these ceremonies is lacking, as is demonstrated by the diverse terminology in the following rites.

Although covenantal rites should provide room for flexibility and adaptation, they should strive to reflect the couple's ethnic, cultural, and personal situation without compromising either partner's individuality. The bottom line is, of course, to do what feels joyful and appropriate for you and your partner. The following rites demonstrate different approaches taken by gay and lesbian couples who have pledged their love for each other.

A CELEBRATION OF LOVE AND COMMITMENT

Chris R. Glaser

Prelude

Couple's Entrance

(*The couple walks down the aisle and meets the presiding minister at the Communion table. A witness for each may stand alongside.*)

Welcome

MINISTER: We gather at the invitation of N. and N. to celebrate their love and commitment in a service to worship God, who blesses all that is good within us.

Our most intimate relations are the text of spirituality, whether between a human being and God, a parent and a child, among believers, or between lovers. Therefore it is appropriate that we lift to God and the community of faith this couple in a public affirmation of the sacred within their intimacy.

Because our world and the church frequently ostracize rather than honor the love of a woman for a woman and a man for a man, this rite of holy intimacy serves as prophetic defiance, as well as public affirmation.

In a world where love may be offered without commitment, and commitments may be made without love, we give thanks to God, whose own steadfast love inspires the integration and integrity of love and commitment of these souls.

Let us pray.

Creator of love,
love that sculpted our bodies,
inspirited our souls,
called us to companionship,
and made us your family:

Bless us, gathered today
as the community in which N. and N.
may be supported and upheld as a couple,
as the family in which N. and N.

may enjoy the freedom to be themselves,
as the church in which N. and N.
may feel your divine welcome
pronounced on all that is good.

In making your Word flesh,
you hallow our bodies,
transform water to wine,
and love us without measure.

Now through your Spirit,
you hear our sighs too deep for words,
sighs of loving and of longing,
sighs of body and soul.
Amen.

Hymn

(*Tune: Joanna, "Immortal, Invisible, God Only Wise," lyrics* © *Chris R. Glaser.*)

All-loving, embracing, God of our hearts,
You hurt with us, laugh with us, teach us your arts;
Your sacred creation you give us to tend
And then your own flesh and spirit you send.

Great giver of mercy and author of love,
Bless those who would follow your long-suffering love:
The Lover you gave us we nailed to a tree,
But Love resurrected in your victory.

Emblazoned in heavens, embodied in earth,
God, bless those who love with repeated rebirth
Past brutal rejections to welcomes of love
And blessings from you—the descent of a dove.

Scriptures
1 John 4:7–12, 18–21; 1 Corinthians 13:4–8a, 13

Homily

Exchange of Vows

(*The couple takes turns reading the sentences.*)
Our love is not simply of the mind,
    but of the heart.
Our love is not simply of the soul,
    but of the body.
Our love lifts us to the heavens,
    yet is rooted deep within the earth.
Our love offers a lifetime and beyond,
    one day at a time.
Our love opens wide our arms
    and focuses our faithfulness.
Our love relinquishes demands
    and offers its best hopes.
Our love creates a home
    and crafts a family.
Our love consecrates a sanctuary for each other
    and for all we hold dear.
Our love glorifies the One who made us
    and the saints who shaped us.
Our love thanks the One who first loved us
    and inspired us to love each other.

Exchange of Tokens

(*This may be rings or other tokens of love and commitment. Some may choose to
omit this segment.*)
With this as token,
I offer my love over time,
praying that our history together
will prove fertile for my love
to grow, and blossom, and sow afresh
the seed of love we plant today
so that our harvest together
may multiply a hundredfold.

Minister's Affirmation

MINISTER: In the presence of those who love you,
    by the power of God's love

embodied in your covenant,
you are joined, one to another.
Thanks be to God!

Embrace of Couple

Prayers

LEADER: Let us pray. O God, we confess that we have often cheapened love. We have sentimentalized it, or equated it with mere physical response, or narrowed it to selfish demands and expectations. We confess that we have often loved only those people who return our love or are like us. May we learn to love regardless of return or condition, as you love us. Forgive us for failing to love as you have first loved us.

CONGREGATION: Dear God, we thank you that N. and N. have invited us to celebrate their commitment of love to each other. In a world frightened of commitment, we admire their courage to covenant together, to give each other the gifts of love throughout their life together. May we honor their invitation to us to join them in this ceremony by honoring and giving support to their growing relationship.

May the glow from their union help light our own way in finding meaning-filled love relationships and in discovering new meaning in the love relationships we already enjoy. May we unite with them in their covenant as we commit ourselves to embrace them as a couple and as individuals of unique value in your sight. In the name of Jesus Christ, the one who taught us how to love, we pray. Amen.

Communion

(*Optional*)

Invitation to Reception

(*Optional*)

Hymn

(*Tune: Nun Danket, "Now Thank We All Our God," lyrics © Chris R. Glaser.*)

Now thank we all our God
For giving our love voices
And hearts to join its song,

In this, our God rejoices,
For this, a cov-e-nant—
A blessing for our world—
Vows proudly said beneath
A rainbow flag unfurled.

We praise our wondrous God
For giving us this moment
Of water turned to wine,
And wine into atonement,
For body, blood bestowed
Not only from above,
But from the flesh of earth
Comes God's redemptive love.

Parting Blessing

Philippians 4:4, 6–7

Postlude

A SAMPLE SERVICE OF HOLY UNION
BASED ON THE TRADITION OF KWANZAA

Darlene Garner

Welcome

PRESIDER: N. and N. would like to welcome you to their Service of Holy Union. They are honored that you could be here to share with them in one of the happiest days of their lives as they become life partners.

(*For an African-American couple:*)

In celebration of their common heritage . . .

(*For interracial couples or if neither partner is African-American:*)

In celebration of the rich gifts shared with us by African-American people . . .

their special ceremony will incorporate elements of Kwanzaa. Kwanzaa is a unique cultural festival that springs from the rich cultural roots of Americans of African ancestry. It is truly fitting that N. and N.

pay such tribute to [their] past[1] and the fruits of their love while taking this important step toward their future. They have asked that you be allowed to share in their ceremony. To each of you individually and to each couple involved in a loving relationship, they extend their love, gratitude, and blessings.

Greeting

PRESIDER: We are gathered here today before God, our ancestors, and friends to celebrate this holy union. We are gathered to rejoice in the gift of love that our Creator shares with us. We affirm today that God who is both Mother and Father desires us to fully experience our humanity. None of us can truly be an island isolated without need of community with others. We offer praise and thanks to God who has blessed us with the wonder of life, breath, hearts, minds, and souls. We rejoice in the realization that we are most alive when we wholeheartedly embrace the gifts that God has given us, especially God's gift of love in all the ways that gift is bestowed.

Opening Prayer

PRESIDER: Let us pray. We do not seek your presence, O God, but rather we acknowledge it. You have declared through your creation that you are present when we gather together; we affirm that you are among us now. Help us to be conscious of your activity as we celebrate. Let your special blessing be upon N. and N. as they declare their covenant with each other. Bless their ancestors, families, and friends. We each seek to be blessed in the name of all that is holy. So be it. Amen.

Readings

1 Corinthians 13; Ruth 1:16–18; or Song of Songs 4:1–7

READER (*concludes the readings*): These are the words of God and of wisdom. Those who live in love, live in God and God in them.

Charge to the Couple

PRESIDER: N. and N., to create a life together with the blessing of God requires that you honor the divine in each other and in yourself; that

---

1. ". . . to their past" should be modified depending upon the cultural background of the couple. Consider substituting ". . . to N.'s past" or omitting this phrase.

you honor the many voices of the soul—the joys, the delights, the love, as well as the anger, the fear, the illness, and the unhealed wounds; that you not ask your life partner to be any less than the fully powerful, proud *woman/man* that *she/he* is; that you embrace *her/him* in *her/his* complexity—in *her/his* delights, in the fullness of *her/his* dreams, in *her/his* relationship with God. This is both God's blessing and charge to you: to live together with honor, courage, and honesty. Are you prepared to accept this challenge?

COUPLE: Yes, we are.

Charge to the Witnesses

PRESIDER: An African proverb teaches us that it takes a village to raise a child. Though they are no longer children, it is still true that it will take a community of friends to support this couple. You stand here representing this couple's friends. So, having heard N. and N. state their intentions to each other and to God in this Service of Holy Union, before God do you pledge to support their union and to strengthen their lives together, to speak the truth to them in love, and with them to seek a life of love for others?

WITNESSES: Yes, we do.

Exchange of Vows

PRESIDER: The traditional celebration of Kwanzaa centers on the *Nguzo Saba*, the seven principles by which African-Americans live in order to further the process of true liberation. The *Nguzo Saba* are social principles that deal with the ways people relate to one another and participate in rebuilding the lives of the community in a self-determined image. In keeping with this tradition and to symbolize their commitment to support one another and to strengthen their relationship as well as their community, N. and N. will now exchange vows that are based upon these principles.

(*Seven candles will be lighted: one black, three red, and three green. The black candle should be lighted first and placed in the center with the red candles on one side of it and the green candles on the other.*)

PRESIDER: N. and N. will now light the first candle. It is the candle of *Umoja*, unity. All other candles will be lighted from this sign of unity for they light this candle to symbolize the unity of all peoples and, especially today, the unity of their lives together. May God be with them in unity and in peace.

(*The presider states and explains each of the principles of Kwanzaa. The couple then responds by reciting their vows in unison.*)

PRESIDER: *Kujichagulia*: self-determination. To define oneself and freely decide one's own fate or course of action, rather than accepting what others say about you.

COUPLE: I promise that I will honor you for who you know yourself to be. With love in my heart, I will always respect and support you as you determine who you will yet become.

PRESIDER: *Ujima:* collective work and responsibility. To work together as a community, trusting one another and remembering that unless everyone benefits, nobody benefits.

COUPLE: I promise that I will be family with you. Working together, there is nothing that we cannot do.

PRESIDER: *Ujamaa*: cooperative economics. To build and to maintain one's own business and economic base in the community and share in all its work and wealth.

COUPLE: I promise that I will do everything within my power to stay economically self-sufficient and yet to share all that I have with you.

PRESIDER: *Nia*: purpose. To strive to build the community as a collective vocation in order to restore the people to their traditional greatness.

COUPLE: I promise that I will set goals with you and work with you to achieve our goals so that our family will have success.

PRESIDER: *Kuumba*: creativity. To exercise one's imagination and originality in pursuit of beauty in order to produce a community that enhances well-being.

COUPLE: I promise that I will create a beautiful and mutually beneficial life with you.

PRESIDER: *Imani*: faith. To believe confidently in the value and trustworthiness of oneself, the ancestors, the present community, the generations yet to come, and the Creator.

COUPLE: I promise that I will share with you my faith in God, in myself and in you.

Blessing of Rings

PRESIDER: These rings mark a milestone on a life journey. From this day you walk toward a horizon that is there but never comes. Your journey will be filled with wonder, surprises, laughter, tears, celebration, grief, and joy. May these rings be a sign to you of the continuing love you pledge here to each other.

Let us pray: Bless, O Holy One, the giving of these rings so that those who wear them may live in your peace and continue in your favor all the days of their lives. So be it. Amen.

Exchange of Rings

COUPLE (*each recites in turn*):
N., I give you this ring
as a sign of my love
and commitment to you
as my life partner
now and always.
Wear it as a reminder
of our trust and faith
in each other
and in our relationship.

Pastoral Prayer

PRESIDER: Let us pray: O God, we pray that this couple and all who are gathered here will grow in the understanding and experience of love. To your tender and watchful care we commit N. and N. In health and sickness, in abundance and want, in life and death, abide with them that they shall never draw away from their love or from you. In the name of all that is holy, we pray. So be it. Amen.

(*The next step is optional. Some couples have given each of their guests a scroll containing a poem of their choice; others have given stones collected at a place special to the couple. It is intended that the* zawadi *be simple and from the heart—which does not have to mean expensive!*)

Sharing of *Zawadi* (Gifts)

PRESIDER: Traditionally, *zawadi*, or gifts, are given on each day of Kwanzaa as a reward for commitments made and kept and are usually exchanged among members of a nuclear family. You are both family and community to this couple, so N. and N. will present each person here with *zawadi* as an expression of their love for you.

Holy Communion

PRESIDER: N. and N., your ancestors came here to this land, lived, loved, struggled, and built here. On these shores, their love and labor rose like the sun and gave strength and meaning to the day. For those who gave so much, you give in return.

For Queen Nzingka and all the others, known and unknown, who defended our ancestral land, history, and humanity from alien invaders.

For Harriet Tubman, Sojourner Truth, Fannie Lou Hamer, Mary McLeod Bethune, Shirley Chisholm, Barbara Jordan, Angela Davis, Audre Lorde, Pat Parker, Michelle Parkerson, Barbara Smith, and all others who dare to define, defend, and develop our interests as a people.[2]

For those who will come after us and for the fuller and freer lives they will have because we continue the struggle.

For the commitment we have made here this day—N. and N. to each other and us to them—which gives identity, purpose, and direction to all our lives.

For the new world we struggle to build.

And for the continuing struggle with which N. and N. will inevitably rescue and reconstruct their history and humanity in their own image and according to their own needs.

On this same soil from this day forward, you will sow your seeds of love, and build and move in unity and strength. Here, too, you will continue your struggle for liberation and a higher level of human life in relationship with each other. Know that you will not struggle in vain. The success of your struggle will be assured because you will walk into your future not only together but also with all of us here today, and with Christ.

Words of Institution

Invitation to Communion

Declaration of Holy Union

PRESIDER: Now that N. and N. have pledged themselves to each other by solemn vows, with the joining of hands and the giving and receiving of rings, I announce to you that they are life partners in the name of God beyond us, God within us, and God between us. Those whom God has joined together, let no one put asunder.

---

2. If this Service of Holy Union is conducted for a male couple, substitute the names of historical and contemporary men whose life work reflects the context.

Today is a new beginning in the lives of these two. May God's grace and love go with you always as you together travel life's journey. May your eyes be like the eagle's, your strength be like the elephant's, and the boldness of your life be like the lion's. And may you remember and honor your ancestors and the legacy they left for you as long as the sun shines and the waters flow.

You may now jump the broom.[3]

CELEBRATION AND BLESSING OF A COVENANTED UNION

Eleanor L. McLaughlin

The Address to the Community

CELEBRANT: We gather here, a community of friends, before the Holy One and in the presence of the Holy in each other, to witness, celebrate, and support the covenant of N. and N. to live together in lifelong love, friendship, and mutual service with the larger human family. The calling to a covenanted life of faithful and self-giving love is a grace and gift from God, in whose image we are created and by whom we are called to love and reason, work and play, to be still and to know ecstasy, to risk and to trust, to receive and to act. Before God we acknowledge our response to this invitation to live in union and harmony with God, with each other, and with all of creation. In celebrating this covenant, we are reminded of and experience our highest vocation: to love God, to love ourselves, and to love neighbor and stranger as ourselves.

God has given us a sign and promise of everlasting love in the rainbow after the flood; in the loyal affection of Jonathan and David; in the steadfast loyalty of Ruth and Naomi; in the recognition that it is God within who unites us, as Elizabeth and Mary were united; in the promise of God's friendship seen in Jesus' embrace of John, the beloved disciple at the Last Supper; and in the promises of baptism, by which we are made a people, one with each other, in Jesus Christ. So we discern here God-With-Us, in the union of these loving and faithful partners, God sealing in hope their vow and covenant with each other as lovers, and with the world, as justice-makers.

---

3. This could be a standard, old-fashioned kitchen broom. Tradition holds that the couple then takes this broom home and sweeps their floor with it to signify sweeping away bad memories and painful things from their past, thereby clearing the way for a clean future together.

Now N. and N. come to stand with each other, surrounded and supported by their family and friends in this community, that in this spring of seasons bright, they may make vows of faithful life together. This covenant and union is intended to be for them a mutual joy, a support in hard times, a comfort in their shared delights. From this union of love and friendship emerges a new family, source of care for the world, the lonely, the lost; a sign for all who see them, that faithfulness and mutual affection triumph over selfishness, egotism, greed, and violence.

We celebrate with them this new family, a "Little Commonwealth," haven and mission of good energy for the healing of the world. Therefore, these mutual promises are to be undertaken and affirmed seriously, reverently, and in accordance with the patterns of truth, beauty, and goodness that enable each to say to the other, "I will you to be." In their commitment, we see the very face of God, a sign of hope and wholeness for all of creation.

N. and N., what do you seek?

COUPLE: We seek a blessing of God, each other, our friends and family, and this community upon our covenant.

Reading

From *Our Passion for Justice: Images of Power, Sexuality and Liberation* by Carter Heyward

Presentation and Witness of
Friends and Family

CELEBRANT: Let us hear the witness and story of those who present and support N. and N. in this commitment.

(*Friends and members of the two families share anecdotes from the past that connect to the present experience of N. and N. and point toward their future.*)

Readings

Song of Solomon and 1 Corinthians 13:1–13

Homily

Statement of Intention

CELEBRANT (*addressing each separately*): Do you, N., choose N. as lifelong partner in this covenanted union?

Do you, N., seek to love N. with all your heart and soul and mind and body?

Will you, N., be for N. a loyal, trustworthy, and faithful partner?

Will you, N., risk in vulnerability to love N. as *she/he* is, to will *her/him* to be *her/his* best self?

Will you, N., give your whole and true self to this relationship, that it may become a growing, healthy, and expansive source of love for yourselves and all who know you?

If you both will make this your intention before this community and before God, respond with a wholehearted, "We will and we do."

The Exchange of Vows

(*Vows are written by the couple and said facing each other with hands clasped and bound by a stole or other symbolic cord.*)

The Blessing and Exchange of Rings

(*The rings are presented and the celebrant blesses them.*)

CELEBRANT: Bless, O Holy God, these rings to be a symbol and reminder of the vows by which these *women/men* pledge themselves to be for and with each other a new family in the midst of the human family. May the Spirit fill N. and N., who wear these rings with the splendor of growing love, and embody their act of faith, hope, and love in a unity of mind, body, and spirit. Amen.

The Ring Words

(*The ring words are composed by the couple. N. takes N.'s ring, puts it on her/his finger and repeats the words of commitment symbolized by the ring. These actions are then repeated by the other partner.*)

The Pronouncement

(*Gathered family and friends may lay their hands on the couple's shoulders. The celebrant may lay her/his hands on their heads.*)

CELEBRANT: Now that N. and N. have given themselves to each other by solemn vows, with the joining and binding of hands and the giving and receiving of rings, may the holy God who indwells in the heavens, the earth, and seas, and the heart and spirit of every creature bless this union in the presence of this community. May God be seen in their life together; may the love between them grow and flourish; and may they be a unity at peace with themselves and with all of creation, for the sake of the world. Those whom God has joined and blessed, let no one put asunder.

Prayer

CELEBRANT: Let us be at prayer.

O Holy One, creator and life-fire of all that is, giver of all healing and wholeness, grace and power. Look with favor upon the world you have made and loved, and for which you pour out your God-life, and look especially upon these two *women/men* whom you join together as one flesh, one mind, one heart. Amen.

Give them wisdom and devotion in the ordering of their common life, that each may be to the other a strength in need, a counselor in perplexity, a comfort in sorrow, and a companion in joy. Amen.

Give them grace, when they hurt each other, to recognize and acknowledge their fault and to seek each other's forgiveness and yours. Amen.

Give them such fulfillment of their mutual affection that they may reach out in love and concern for others. Amen.

Grant that all of us, who in hope and faith live in the freedom and responsibility of vowed life together, may find our lives strengthened and our loyalties confirmed. Amen.

Music or Poem

The Blessing of
the Covenanted Union

CELEBRANT: Creator God, hovering and indwelling Spirit, you made us not for loneliness but to dwell together in mutual and faithful affection. Bless and keep N. and N. that they may honor each other in all times and places. Let the sacred fire of friendship burn brighter between them. Let their love deepen and widen and be as a rich garden bed of every flower and fruit. Let forgiveness end any disputes, humor unburden them in the midst of difficulty, and holy service to the world be the true riches they seek. Now, O Holy Wisdom, give your grace and nurture to N. and N. May your birth-giving be a blessing of light and warmth in their lives that they continue to grow in joy with each other and as a reconciling presence in your world. Amen.

Candle Ceremony

(*Celebrant presents N. and N. each with a lighted candle. N. and N. together light a single larger candle from which the assembly takes individual lights.*)

CELEBRANT: From every human being there rises a light reaching out toward heaven. When two souls that are called to become one flesh choose each other, their streams of light flow together and a single brighter light goes forth from their united being.

Dismissal

CELEBRANT: Let us dance as David danced, laugh as Sarah laughed, and go in peace and light to set the world on fire. Alleluia, alleluia, alleluia.

COVENANT RITE

Zalmon Sherwood

(*The worship setting is a room in a home that is decorated for a festive occasion. Background music may be played as the guests greet one another and the couple. The couple invite the guests to be seated while the couple remain standing.*)

ONE PARTNER: We stand here today in the presence of people from so many parts of our journeys. You are the people who have been family for us.

OTHER PARTNER: We have brought this community of friends and colleagues together to witness and celebrate the beginning of a new part of our journey. We are here to make a covenant together.

COMMUNITY: We rejoice to be part of this occasion. We have loved and valued you separately. We will continue to love and value you in relationship.

(*Members of the community may offer statements of reflection about the couple.*)

OFFICIANT: In the midst of our most hopeful and joyful times, we remember that we are human beings who miss the mark of God's high calling for abiding love. We must never forget the pain and heartbreak that are even now a part of our lives and the life of the world as a whole. While we are celebrating this union, others are enduring the pain of separation. While we are enjoying a feast this day, others are starving because of the way in which we humans have divided the world's goods. Help us, God, to be ever mindful of the needs of this world. Help us to see this covenant we celebrate today as formed not only to bring greater joy and happiness to the persons involved but also to direct outward concern and care for all sisters and brothers.

ALL: We are a community, with songs aching to be sung, with words aching to be spoken, with questions aching to be answered, with feelings aching to be expressed, with hearts aching for love, with arms aching for embracing.

(*Music or dance is appropriate here. Following a period of silence, the couple rise to recite the following covenant. Instead of holding hands, they touch each other's chest and speak directly from their hearts.)*

ONE PARTNER: Out of all the people and places in my life, it is you with whom I choose to be in a special covenant. It is you whom I have chosen to rearrange my life around and with. I celebrate the gift of this relationship and the work of giving that gift.

OTHER PARTNER: Of all the people I have known on my journey, it is you with whom I choose to journey on this covenant. With you and your life I choose to weave the strands of my life. I celebrate the gift of this relationship and the work of receiving that gift.

ONE PARTNER: I love you, N., and I want to give you the best of who I am and who I am becoming. I choose to live in covenant with you. I know that journey will not be easy, but I live better when I live with you.

OTHER PARTNER: I promise to work, to play, to dream with you and to do my best to make those dreams come true. I promise to share your tears and your laughter and to allow you to share mine. I promise to respect the need of both of us to have separate space and to come back to you as I trust you will come back to me. I promise to respect you and to celebrate the ways you are different from me. I promise to seek your forgiveness when we have failed to live up to our covenant.

(Following this exchange, the couple may kiss and embrace. A musical selection may follow. After a period of silence, the following litany is recited:)

OFFICIANT: Because our love for one another is often not recognized, because our commitments are not legal,

ALL: We witness your commitment to one another. We validate your love, and support you in your lives together. We testify that today you have bravely formed an authentic, important bond, worthy of respect.

OFFICIANT: Because our families often reject us, because our children can legally be taken from us,

ALL: We accept you as a new family. We will appreciate and respect our new families on par with the old. We admire your courage and cherish you as family.

OFFICIANT: Because we are often made invisible, because our history is often hidden, altered, or destroyed,

ALL: We celebrate the beauty of this ceremony and your love. We praise and honor your strength. We will remember and celebrate the anniversary of this day. We will document our lives together.

OFFICIANT: Because we have often been attacked by hatred, because we have often been ridiculed as crazy, deluded, or sick,

ALL: We vow to protect you as a couple. We will nourish and defend your love for each other. We will shelter one another from those who hate. Our shield will be forged from our openness to ourselves and to our love.

OFFICIANT: Because we so often internalize our oppression in self-destructive behaviors,

ALL: We will share truths with one another. We will help you realize your goals of personal growth toward self-love and value.

OFFICIANT: Because we are called evil, sinners, wicked; because we have been imprisoned and psychoanalyzed to punish our love,

ALL: We bless and sanctify your relationship. We admire your dedication to each other. We exalt the purity and holiness of your love.

(*After a period of silent meditation, the officiant continues.*)

OFFICIANT: We give thanks, Loving and Holy One, for the joy of this day, deeper than human words; for the strength of this moment and the graceful presence of a beloved community; and for the powerful embrace of human hearts. Especially do we celebrate before you the goodness of the covenant between N. and N. May they create a life inhabited by your love, and a home in which no one is a stranger. Defend them from every danger, and lead them into all peace. Bless them in their companionship, and when their time together on earth is over, grant that they may look back in joy at lives well lived, hearts mended, justice honored, mercy done, and the world transformed by the witness of their love.

ALL:

We will not be afraid to dance our dreams anymore.

We will not be afraid to say what we know anymore.

We will not be afraid to say whom we love anymore.

We have claimed past tears and lost dreams.

We have entered into a new covenant and tasted its goodness.

We will not be afraid. We will not be afraid.

THE WEDDING: A DEMONSTRATION FOR
THE RIGHTS OF LESBIAN, GAY, AND BI COUPLES

Troy D. Perry

I created "The Wedding" as a massive, nonsectarian ceremony of commitment and demonstration for couples' rights in conjunction with the 1993 March on Washington for Lesbian, Gay, and Bi Equal Rights and Liberation. At least 2,600 couples participated in "The Wedding" on April 24, 1993, in front of the Internal Revenue Service building in Washington, D.C. Couples were asked to bring with them a ring, necklace, bracelet, pin, or other memento to give each other as a sign of their mutual affection. Before the ceremony, the crowd cheered as they listened to speeches from a variety of speakers who have been on the front lines fighting for the rights of lesbian, gay, and bisexual couples in the United States.

The ceremony itself was one of the most moving that I have ever had the honor of conducting, and I hope that it becomes a model for similar demonstrations across the United States and throughout the world.

Introduction

PRESIDER: Dearly beloved, we gather together here to stand before our friends, the larger society, and the United States government to proclaim our committed relationships. We do not make this proclamation lightly, but reverently, discreetly, and soberly. We stand before our nation and our friends because we wish to proclaim our right to love one another. We stand here knowing that love makes a family—nothing else, nothing less! We stand here knowing of the lies and untruths that have been told about us by some in the larger community. But we stand here pure of heart and unafraid in proclaiming that our concern and care for one another is as rich as that in any culture or community. It is with glad hearts this day that we stand in the light to proclaim our love one for another. We will no longer be silent about the love that dare not speak its name. We do this without hesitation in the full knowledge that we owe apologies to no one. We stand here today because we care. We stand today, many of us, in the valley of the shadow of death, realizing that this may be the last time we get to pledge our love one to the other in a public forum.

We who are part of our community remember an ancient story in which two women pledged their love to each other. One woman said to the other, "Do not ask me to leave you or to return and quit following after you, for where you go, I will go, and where you live, I will live. Your family will be my family, and your God shall be my God. Where you die, I will die, and there I will be buried. Only death shall part you and me." Ruth and Naomi stuck together through great adversity. They traveled a long distance to stay together, looked after each other, and protected each other from danger. They expressed their love through physical affection in kissing and holding each other. They respected family and community customs and still retained the integrity of their love.

We know of another ancient story of two men who did the same. Upon the death of Jonathan, David swore his eternal love for Jonathan and stated in 2 Sam. 1:26 that his love for Jonathan surpassed the love he had for the opposite sex.

I remember the words spoken by lesbian feminist activist Kate Millet in Los Angeles in 1978, when she said, "Never forget the nights of your love and the days of working for its freedom, its expansion to fill the world with the roses of those moments out of time. An army of lovers makes a revolution."

It is on that foundation that we come today to again emphatically state our love one for another. We realize the prejudice that still exists in our culture concerning our right to live together, but we gladly challenge such prejudice rather than retreat into the shadows of despair and ignorance. We will not be stopped as we take our rightful place in this country as children of America. We shall be heard!

Ceremony

PRESIDER: Participants, is it your desire to take your vows of commitment at this time? If so, please respond, "It is."

As you are standing before me, couples, will the member of the couple who is standing to my right turn to your partner and do two things. First, tell them why you love them, and second, tell them why this ceremony is important to you.

I asked before this ceremony that each of you bring a token of your covenant. At this time I would ask that the individual member of the couple to my right take the gift, whether it is a ring, bracelet, pin, or other token—even if it is just a kiss of your affection—repeat after me, and then give your token of affection to your partner:

PARTICIPANT AND PRESIDER (*alternately*): I give you this gift as a token of our covenant,

    vowing to live together in close friendship and love,

    and to strive for fuller knowledge of your being

    and to care for you above all others.

    I pledge myself to recognize your needs

and to encourage your full potential
and to love you even as I love myself.
May love dwell between you and me forever.
(*Repeat with the member of the couple to the left.*)

PRESIDER: Forasmuch as each of these couples have declared their love one for the other and have given tokens of their covenant each to the other, and have done this willingly before their friends gathered here, as well as before the larger American community, we proclaim together our rights as couples in hope that the day will come when not only will our own community recognize our relationships, but the laws of our country will also.

Couples, you may kiss.

7

Rites of
Holy Communion

Holy Communion is a sacred meal recognized as the primary liturgy of Christianity. The ceremony originated with Jesus Christ who, just prior to his arrest and crucifixion, shared bread and wine as his body and blood with his disciples.

Christian denominations celebrate Holy Communion in a variety of ways. Many religious traditions refer to Communion as Eucharist, from the Greek word meaning "Thanksgiving." Some churches celebrate Holy Communion each week while others observe the rite once a month or simply several times a year. Eucharistic elements vary from bread to wafers to crackers, from wine to grape juice.

Holy Communion traditionally has been an exclusionary rite. In some churches only baptized members with a certain level of religious education and "morality" are welcome to receive Communion, and only an ordained minister is allowed to preside over the sacred meal. Ordination is still not available to women or openly gay men and lesbians in many denominations.

The following rites provide more inclusive models for Holy Communion, during which all seekers are welcome to share in Christ's passion, to partake of Christ's life and love, and to go forth refreshed and empowered for ministry.

EUCHARISTIC PRAYER FOR
THE POWERLESS, THE OPPRESSED, THE UNUSUAL

Marilyn McCord Adams

CELEBRANT: Our God is here.

PEOPLE: God's Spirit is with us.

CELEBRANT: Unlock the doors of your hearts.

PEOPLE: We open them to God and to one another.

CELEBRANT: We have come to meet God, our Friend and our Lover.

PEOPLE: It is good to love God, now and always.

CELEBRANT: It is good to live as lovers of God with brothers and sisters in all times and places. Therefore, with those who befriended and fed you, who argued with you and touched you, who got angry with you and saw your face, who ran away from you only to meet you on their path, we praise you saying:

ALL: Holy, holy, vulnerable God,
> God of love and joy,
> heaven and earth are full of your blessing;
> stay with us always.
> Blessed is the One
> who comes in the name of our God,
> who makes our hearts glad.

CELEBRANT: God of the powerless, the oppressed, the unusual,
> we praise you for your special love
> for those who somehow don't fit in.

> Your Spirit calmed the storm-tossed deep,
> Your Word shaped chaos into a world,
> which you called GOOD.

> You formed your people Israel from refugees and slaves,
> turned nobodies into somebodies,
> by giving them your family name.

> You taught us survival in wilderness places,
> fed us with unknown manna,
> quenched our thirst with water from the rock,
> over and over showed yourself entirely trustworthy,
> yet full of surprises.

> You brought us into the land you had prepared for us,
> to be a holy community with room for everyone
> to grow and stretch, create and love

111

to the praise of your name.

Your fatherly guidance, motherly teaching, were
to welcome exiles and strangers,
to care for the weak and poor,
to visit the sick and elderly,
all a trademark of your love.

But we forgot that we were slaves in Egypt.
We demanded to be like other nations,
to organize the world for our convenience,
to lord it over the have-nots,
to reject the defective and the different as unclean.

Time and again, your warning prophets
were rejected as traitors.
In exile and hardship you got our attention,
but we always went home to shut others out.
Yet our resistance could never defeat your dream.

You came among us as outcast, illegitimate, exiled.
You touched lepers and bleeding women,
ate with tax collectors, recruited prostitutes,
healed the tormented, taught the hopeless,
picked unstable and unlikely disciples,
welcomed North and South, East and West
to the marriage feast of the Lamb.

On the night before you died for us,
you took bread, gave thanks, broke it,
and gave it to your friends, saying:
Take, eat: This is my body which is given for you.
Do this for the remembrance of me.

After supper, you took the cup of wine,
gave thanks, and gave it to them, saying:
Drink this, all of you: This is my blood of the new covenant,
poured out for you and for everyone for the forgiveness of sins.
Whenever you drink it, do this for the remembrance of me.

Yearning to please you, O God:
We remember your death for us, your friends.
We shout your resurrection, our bold new life.
Come, sweet Jesus, embrace us face to face.

And we set the table with gifts from our world,
this bread and this wine,

our brothers and sisters who live and die with AIDS,
our disappointments and failures,
the harms we have suffered and the grief we have caused.

By your Holy Spirit may they become for us
the bread of life and the cup of salvation,
your body and blood,
that we may love as your body in the world.

Remember your holy family, and especially this parish:
its founders who sounded your praise when movies were silent,
brave Filipinos and Latinos starting over in a new land,
gay and lesbian persons giving birth to new identities,
church-damaged, excluded, and unusual people,
seeking the power of your kiss, the strength of your love.

Bind us together with all your saints past and yet to come;
send us out to help others recognize themselves as your children;
transform your church, our city and planet,
into wholesome community, as wide and deep as your love. Amen.

THE GREAT THANKSGIVING: A RITE BASED ON THE SONG OF MARY

Carter Heyward

(*This rite is based on Luke 1:47–55.*)

CELEBRANT: May God be with you.

PEOPLE: And also with you.

CELEBRANT: Open your hearts.

PEOPLE: We open them to God.

CELEBRANT: Let us give thanks to God.

PEOPLE: It is right to give God thanks and praise.

CELEBRANT: It is a right and joyful thing to stand in the presence of God and one another, trusting as we do that where the Spirit of God moves among us, we are beckoned as lovers to present ourselves as partners in the holy work of creation and redemption, for God's sake and for our own.

PEOPLE: We proclaim your greatness, O God. We rejoice in you, our Savior.

CELEBRANT: We rejoice in you, merciful Father, for remembering us, even in our forgetfulness of you. We give thanks to you, patient Mother, for remembering us, even in our dis-memberment of you.

PEOPLE: For your regard has blessed us, ordinary men and women who serve you. As you have blessed us, so too will all generations remember us as your people.

CELEBRANT: We your people, whom you have chosen as friends, recall the splendid array of gifts you have set before us: the breath and sensuality of our bodies; the food on our tables; the warmth and comfort of shelter; the support and solidarity of friends; the intimacy of lovers, family, those who reach out to us even in our fear and denial.

PEOPLE: You, strong Friend, have raised us up to befriend. Touched and moved by your power, we are empowered to love the world you have made. Because your power is great, so too is the power of your friends.

CELEBRANT: Gathered in friendship, we remember what you have done to bring us here: we remember your commitment to your people, your commandment that we love one another, your liberation of our forebears from injustice and oppression, your steadfast promise that you will not forget us.

PEOPLE: Your mercy is on those who fear you throughout all generations. You have showed strength with your arm.

CELEBRANT: But most of all, you have shown compassion toward us and all humankind. You have shown that you are with us and that your movement can be ours as well. This we see in Jesus, our brother, our friend, our savior, for we remember his life, death, and resurrection as a sign and a promise that your love cannot be crushed, your justice cannot be undone, your ways cannot be thwarted, and your life cannot be taken away, as long as we your people are faithful to you in the same spirit that Jesus Christ was your faithful son.

PEOPLE: You have scattered the proud in their hearts' fantasy. You have put down the mighty from their seat and have lifted up the powerless.

CELEBRANT: We remember, O God of Power, that your son Jesus, on the night before he died for us, took bread, blessed it, and gave it to his friends, and said, "Take, eat; this is my body, which is given for you. Do this in remembrance of me." After supper, he took the cup of wine, blessed it, and gave it to them, and said, "Drink this, all of you. This is my blood of the new covenant, which will be shed for you. Whenever you drink it, remember me."

PEOPLE: We remember his passion, O God, and your justice: that you fill the hungry with good things and send the rich, empty, away.

CELEBRANT: We are hungry people, and so we ask you, O God of justice and mercy, to bless this bread and this wine, making them for us the body and blood of Jesus Christ, in whose Spirit we are called and sanctified to live holy lives.

PEOPLE: You, gracious God, remembering your mercy, have helped your people in all generations, as you promised Abraham, Sarah, and Hagar; now stand with us, blessing those who share this feast of love, that we may go forth from this place, empowered to join with you in your ongoing creation, liberation, and blessing of the world.

ALL: All this we ask in the name of Jesus Christ. Feed us daily, hold us fast, send us forth boldly, joyfully, and ever faithful in your Spirit. Amen.

And now in the Spirit of Christ we pray:

Our Father, Our Mother, you are in heaven. Holy is your name. Your justice come. Your will be done on earth as in heaven. Give us today the bread we need. And forgive us our sins as we forgive those who sin against us. Save us from the time of trial, and deliver us from evil. For the goodness, the power and the glory are yours, now and forever. Amen.

DIGNITY/USA CONVENTION EUCHARIST 1991

James E. Snight Jr., adapted by *Kevin Calegari* and *Thomas Kaun*

While these prayers are not explicitly "lesbigay," they are explicit in Dignity members' self-understanding, appropriating biblical images for liberative purposes and expressing solidarity with all oppressed peoples. They are also quite orthodox and include all the prescribed forms for a canonically valid Roman Eucharist.

This Eucharist was originally written for three voices and designed for extensive overlap and interplay among the voices. It was concelebrated at the 1991 Dignity/USA Biennial Convention in Washington, D.C., by a priest, a laywoman, and a layman.

(*The responses may be spoken or sung.*)
ONE: May God be with you.
MANY: And also with you.
ONE: Let us lift up our hearts.
MANY: We have lifted them up.
ONE: Let us give thanks to the living God.
MANY: It is right to give God thanks and praise.

ONE:

    You are a God of justice and peace.

    You are a God of mercy and compassion.

    You are God, living and true.

    We worship,

    We give you thanks,

    We praise you for your glory!

MANY: Praise, thanks, and glory be to you, O God!

ONE: When all was in darkness, you moved upon the water.

    When all was in darkness, you called forth light.

    When all was in darkness, you raised us to life.

MANY: Praise, thanks, and glory be to you, O God!

ONE: You turned the night into day.

    You changed our tears into dancing.

    You formed us in your own loving image.

MANY: Praise, thanks, and glory be to you, O God!

ONE: We are the people of the water.

    We are the children of the light.

    We are the heirs of your everlasting covenant.

MANY: Praise, thanks, and glory be to you, O God!

ONE: Though we speak different languages, in you we are one.

    Though we come from near and far, in you we are one.

    With all our hopes and prayers, in you we are one.

    For in Jesus, we have become your daughters and sons.

    In Jesus, we have become sisters and brothers.

    In Jesus, we have become companions on our pilgrim way to you.

MANY: Praise, thanks and glory be to you, O God!

ONE: United in you, we celebrate the dignity of our lives.

    United in you, we dare to dance, even in the shadow of death.

    United in you, we shall not be silent;

    we join in the great hymn of creation.

MANY: Holy, holy, holy,

    Lord God of power and might.

    Heaven and earth are full of your glory.

    Hosanna in the highest.

    Blessed is the one who comes in the name of the Lord.

    Hosanna in the highest.

ONE: You are holy, the fountain from which flows living water—

    water that quenches our thirst for wholeness,

for holiness, for mercy, for justice,
for freedom, for peace, for love.

MANY: Praise, thanks, and glory be to you, O God!

ONE: In your loving-kindness, you have not abandoned us but forged, through Jesus, a bond that can never be broken.

In your loving-kindness, you have not condemned us but have shown us, through Jesus, your saving love.

In your loving-kindness, you continue to call us, through Jesus, into a life of community, dignity, and love.

MANY: Praise, thanks, and glory be to you, O God!

ONE: May your Spirit, which breathed upon the waters, fill us with your love that we might be a new creation.

May your Spirit open our eyes to the wondrous gifts you have given us in this bread of unity, this cup of love.

May your Spirit empower us to be people of the water and your name.

Gathered here, we remember the love you have shown us.

Gathered here, we celebrate the freedom you have given us.

Gathered here, we believe the promises you have made to us.

MANY: We remember how you loved us, to your death. And still we celebrate, for you are with us here. And we believe that we will see you when you come in your glory, Lord. We remember, we celebrate, we believe.[1]

(*The following Words of Institution are designed for three people to assume alternate roles: One speaks, one signs, and one holds the bread or cup.*)

ONE: We remember the witness Jesus gave:
The outstretched hands that brought healing,
The consoling words that brought hope,
The blessings given to those whose ears were open,
whose hands were open,
whose hearts were open.

We remember the witness Jesus gave:
How, on that last night, he took bread,
blessed it,
broke it, and gave it to the disciples:
"This is my body, which will be given up for you."

MANY: We remember how you loved us, to your death. And still we cele-

---

1. From Marty Haugen, "Mass of Remembrance" (Chicago: G.I.A. Publications, 1987).

brate, for you are with us here. And we believe that we will see you when you come in your glory, Lord. We remember, we celebrate, we believe.

ONE: We remember the witness Jesus gave:

How he took the cup of blessing,

the cup of deliverance,

the cup of memorial,

blessed it, and gave it to the disciples:

"This is the cup of my blood,

the blood of the new and everlasting covenant.

It will be shed for you and for all,

so that sins may be forgiven.

Do this in memory of me."

MANY: We remember how you loved us, to your death. And still we celebrate, for you are with us here. And we believe that we will see you when you come in your glory, Lord. We remember, we celebrate, we believe.

ONE: With grateful hearts we offer this life-giving sacrifice, which reveals to us the depth of your love.

With faithful hearts we bind ourselves in everlasting covenant to be one people.

With exultant hearts we celebrate our great dignity as your daughters and sons.

MANY: We remember how you loved us, to your death. And still we celebrate, for you are with us here. And we believe that we will see you when you come in your glory, Lord. We remember, we celebrate, we believe.

ONE: With hopeful hearts we pray for the day when N., the bishop of Rome, and N., our bishop, will sit at table with us.

With expectant hearts we pray that all who profess Jesus' name will one day celebrate in one communion of love.

With giving hearts we promise to follow Jesus' example and place ourselves in service to all who are in need, so that we might always worship in spirit and in truth.

With loving hearts we commend to your mercy all our sisters and brothers who have died in the hope of rising again.

Welcome them to your eternal banquet, and dry the tears of all who mourn.

MANY: We remember how you loved us, to your death. And still we celebrate, for you are with us here. And we believe that we will see you when you come in your glory, Lord. We remember, we celebrate, we believe.

ONE: Around this table, we remember those who opened the way for us.

Around this table, we celebrate the many gifts you have given us.

Around this table, we come to believe more deeply the unity you have created in us.

As we remember,
as we celebrate,
as we believe,
we pray that through Christ, with Christ, in Christ,
in the unity of the Spirit,
all glory and power be yours now and forevermore.

ALL: Amen!

THE DESERT EXPERIENCE

Christine Nusse

This liturgy was celebrated at the 1992 National Gathering of the Conference for Catholic Lesbians (CCL).

Entrance Song

"Coming Home" by Carolyn McDade

Call to Prayer

LEADER: Like the deer that yearn for running streams,
    so we are thirsting for God, the Living God.
(*Lighting of the Candle/Aspersion*)
LEADER: In the desert we search for the thread of God.
ALL: In the desert we search.
LEADER: Because of who we are,
    we are excluded from the churches and communities.
ALL: In the desert we search for the thread of God.
LEADER: To you, Giver of Life, we call in faith,
    in search of love, and truth, and wholeness.
ALL: Be with us; hear us, we pray.

Readings

Hosea 2:16
"The Thread," from *Poems 1960–67* by Denise Levertov (New York: New Directions Publishing Corp., 1978)

Responsorial Song

Refrain from "The Dreamer, the Tree and Me" by Kathy Sherman

Readings

1 Kings 19:1–15
"Briefly It Enters, and Briefly Speaks" from *The Boat of Quiet Hours* by Jane Kenyon (St. Paul: Graywolf Press, 1986)

Responsorial Song

Refrain from "The Dreamer, the Tree and Me"
by Kathy Sherman

Reflection/Discussion

(*In groups of three to five, discuss the following questions.*)
1. Can I recognize the thread of God in my life?
2. What do I see as obstacles to a fuller spiritual life?
3. If I could dream an ideal spiritual life, what would be happening in that dream?

Universal Prayer

CANTOR: In peace let us pray to our God.
RESPONSE: "Kyrie" of the Taizé community.
CANTOR: For this conference and all those who attend it, and for those who could not be here, let us pray to our God.
ALL: Kyrie eleison.
CANTOR: For CCL communities and CCL members, that we grow in harmony, truth, and love, let us pray . . .
ALL: Kyrie eleison.
CANTOR: For the groups and coalitions that work for justice in the churches, let us pray . . .
ALL: Kyrie eleison.
CANTOR: For our country and those in authority, that they act with justice and compassion, let us pray . . .
ALL: Kyrie eleison.
CANTOR: For the refugees, the homeless, the orphans, that we work at finding true homes for all, let us pray . . .
ALL: Kyrie eleison.
CANTOR: For the sick, for those who suffer in their body, in their mind, or in their spirit, that they find healing, let us pray . . .

ALL: Kyrie eleison.

CANTOR: For the victims of violence between countries, ethnic groups, gangs, city dwellers, family members, that we dare to build peace, let us pray . . .

ALL: Kyrie eleison.

CANTOR: For this earth and each other, that we learn to nurture life and foster love, let us pray . . .

ALL: Kyrie eleison.

CANTOR: For our own needs and those of others, (*pause*) let us pray . . .

ALL: Kyrie eleison.

CANTOR: In the communion of all the saints,
  let us commend ourselves and one another,
  and all our life to Christ our God.

ALL: Kyrie eleison.

Peace

LEADER: The peace of Christ be always with us.
(*Kiss of peace*)

Offertory Song

"Covenant" by Carolyn McDade

Eucharist

LEADER: Ancient love, source of our being and goal of our longing,
  we praise you and give you thanks
  because you have created us,
  women loving women, in your image
  to cherish your world
  and seek your face.

ALL: Rejected by your church's priests and powers,
  cut from our ancestors' faith,
  you do not turn from us.
  On the contrary,
  you call us to seek you
  and love you more intimately.
  In the desert you seduce us
  and speak to our heart.

LEADER: Therefore, with all the women before us
  who were discounted and oppressed,

with our foremothers,
with the saints and angels, we say:
ALL: Holy, holy, holy,
vulnerable God,
heaven and earth are full of your glory;
hosanna in the highest.
Blessed is the one who comes in the name of God;
hosanna in the highest.
LEADER: Blessed is the one you sent, Jesus,
who himself was thrown out of his village,
distrusted by his own people,
betrayed by a close friend,
and handed over to the police
by his church's priests and authorities.
ALL: On the night he was to be arrested
Jesus longed to eat with his friends
the Passover of Hope.
In this last meal,
he took bread, gave thanks, broke it, and said:
"This is my body, which is given for you.
Do this to remember me."
(*Pause.*)
In the same way he took the cup
after supper, saying:
"This cup is the new covenant in my blood.
Do this whenever you drink it in remembrance of me."
(*Singing:*)
Christ has died, alleluia.
Christ is risen, alleluia.
Christ will come again, alleluia, alleluia.
LEADER: Therefore as we eat this bread
and drink this cup,
we are proclaiming Christ's death until he comes.
ALL: In the body broken and blood poured out,
we restore to memory and hope
the broken and unremembered victims
of tyranny and sin,
and particularly today
the victims of sexism and homophobia.

And we long for the bread of tomorrow
and the wine of the age to come.
LEADER: Come then, life-giving Spirit of our God,
brood over these bodily things,
and make us one body with Christ;
that we may labor with creation
to make the desert fruitful
and to build with each other
a true, free, and open community.
ALL: Amen.

Communion Song

"Come, Drink Deep" by Carolyn McDade

Meditation Dance

Liturgical dance while choir sings "This Ancient Love" by Carolyn
McDade

In Lieu of Blessing

Excerpts from "Charge to Women," from *WomanChrist* by Christin Lore
Weber (New York: Harper & Row, 1987)

Final Song

"Trouble and Beauty" by Carolyn McDade
(*Carolyn McDade's tapes and books can be obtained from Carolyn McDade, P.O.
Box 510, Wellfleet, Massachusetts 02667. Kathy Sherman's tapes can be ob-
tained from Sisters of St. Joseph, Dept. M, 1515 Ogden Avenue, LaGrange Park,
Illinois 60625.*)

EARTH COMMUNION

Sylvia Perez

Earth communion has a powerful impact on everyone who participates,
and therefore much thought and prayer should go into deciding when
and where to do it. Choose a location that does not need to be kept
clean, for earth communion is much "earthier" than a traditional
Communion service of bread and juice. An ideal location is outdoors or
at a rustic retreat center where the floor can serve as the altar.

Earth communion is a rite that requires the worship leader to begin both physical and spiritual preparation two or three days in advance. Preparation focuses on making a bowl out of clay. Begin by thinking and praying about the people who will be present for the earth communion: What are their hopes, ideas, fears, and wishes as individuals and as a community? What will they be doing in the days and hours before and after the earth communion?

Keep these questions in your heart and mind as you shape the bowl from the clay. Make the walls of the bowl fairly thin, no more than a quarter of an inch. Leave your thumbprints and finger marks visible, so the bowl looks raw and unfinished. Find a place in your home for the bowl to sit while it is drying. Let the bowl harden so it becomes brittle, but do not fire it. Allow its presence in your home to inspire your reflections on the upcoming rite.

Materials needed for the rite include your handmade clay bowl and a mortar and pestle. You may also want to have a small piece of carpet on which to break the bowl. All of these must be near the worship leader as the rite begins. If others are going to assist in distributing the earth communion, each of them will need a waterproof bowl.

Earth communion begins with everyone sitting in a circle. Preparatory music, readings, and/or prayers may be offered. Then hold the bowl as you share about your preparation with the rest of the group. Describe making the bowl, including your thoughts and feelings as you made it. Mention your own dreams and doubts, as well as those of the people gathered. In a lesbian and gay gathering, describe the dream of a world where everyone is free to love whomever one chooses. Let your emotions come out as you speak.

WORSHIP LEADER: This bowl is an unfinished product, just like us. We're never completely where we want ourselves to be and we probably never will be, however old we get. Things don't always work out the way we want them to. No matter what we think about what we want, sometimes it doesn't happen. And at times things break!

(*Take the bowl and throw it down on the ground to smash it. Be prepared to feel grief and shock yourself and in the congregation.*)

WORSHIP LEADER: No matter what happens to us, we do not have to break. We can find ways to go on even after the breaking of our dreams and hearts and hopes.

(*In a lesbian and gay context, you may want to refer to the brokenness felt when we are rejected by family, church, and society because of our sexual orientation. While you gather the pieces into the mortar and grind them, retell in your own words the Native American story of Lone Eagle printed here.)*

Lone Eagle was a Native American woman who was filled with anger. She had been reprimanded by the chief of the tribe and now felt the stings of embarrassment. Lone Eagle sought to find a way to publicly humiliate the chief.

At the next tribal gathering, Lone Eagle walked into the circle of people with her hands cupped above her head. The other members of the tribe could see that she held a junco, a small bird, because black and white tail feathers were sticking out of her hands. She addressed the chief.

"Tell me, Chief, is this bird dead or is this bird alive?" she challenged. If he said it was dead, she planned to open her hands and let it fly away. If he said it was alive, she would crush the life from it. When she opened her hands, the bird would lie there still for everyone to see. Lone Eagle intended that no matter what the chief said, he would be wrong and she would be vindicated. The whole tribe stood silently, waiting for the chief's reply.

"Lone Eagle," he said, looking straight into her eyes, "it's up to you whether that bird lives or dies."

Never taking her eyes off the chief, Lone Eagle hesitated, then slowly opened her hands to let the bird fly free.

WORSHIP LEADER: Each one of us has the power to decide the direction that our lives are going to take. You decide what the bird means in your life: a relationship, a job, your spirituality, past memories, whatever. You have the choice whether that bird lives or dies. You've got to be willing to take responsibility. There are things in our lives that we should nurture; there are also unhealthy aspects of our lives that we should stop. I invite you to think about what you need to look at in your own life and decide what you need to nurture and what you need to let go.

(Add water to the ground-up pieces of clay and begin mixing it into a watery paste. As you do this, say something like:)

When I first started, I began with clay and made a bowl. It broke, but what I have here is clay again. I could build a bowl again if I wanted, although it would look different from the first bowl. Other things grow from what breaks. We all take part in cycles.

We can miss opportunities. The Chinese word for *crisis* is composed of two characters that mean *opportunity* and *danger*. If we focus too much on the danger, we lose sight of the opportunity in a crisis. There will be times of breaking and crisis. Christ's body was broken, but Christ's spirit lives on and is here with us and in us. God has promised us that the cycle of life will continue.

Everyone here is invited to receive this earth communion in the next few minutes. [*My assistants and*] I will move around the circle and smear some of this clay on each person's cheeks as a sign that we have the power within ourselves to make a difference in our lives and in the lives of others. Breaking just means taking on another form.

(*Participants may want to sing during and after the distribution of earth communion. Appropriate songs include "The Earth Is Our Mother," "The Earth, the Air, the Fire, the Water," "Seek Ye First," "Blessed Assurance," "Simple Gifts" and "Ubi Caritas."*)

(A performance by Omega Peace Arts, a dance troupe in Berkeley, California, provided inspiration for parts of this ritual.)

8

Rites of Lesbian/Gay Pride and Empowerment

Religious ceremonies are often part of the annual lesbian and gay pride celebrations held throughout the United States and elsewhere during the month of June. These events commemorate the June 29, 1969 Stonewall Rebellion, during which lesbians and gay men fought back against police harassment in New York City. Historians point to this date as the birth of the modern lesbian and gay rights movement. Some churches with primarily lesbian and gay membership refer to June as the liturgical season of "Pridetide." However, as the rites in this chapter illustrate, ceremonies of lesbian and gay pride, freedom, and empowerment can be conducted at any time of the year.

Despite discrimination, defeats, and setbacks, lesbians and gay men share with other oppressed minorities the resilience to persevere, to march forward, to struggle toward the day when it will be forevermore wrong to ridicule another human being or cheat a person out of participating in life at its fullest. An important witness of the lesbian and gay community is its ability to celebrate, to savor life, and to recognize individuals who have contributed to the community.

INVOCATION FOR ALL SAINTS' DAY

James Lancaster

LEADER: God of grace and passion, we praise you for your love deep in our hearts. Bring into this assembly the presence of all your lesbian and gay children of every time and place, that we may draw strength and courage from your mighty works in them.

ALL: Yes, Jesus, join us with our sisters and brothers.

LEADER: How wonderful are your ways, O lesbian God; how thrilling the wonders of your creation, for you have endowed your gay and lesbian saints of all times with these gifts of your grace: love, to love each other; endurance, to live that love despite all oppression; courage, to bear your love into the world; hope, to envision a better world, the new creation you have promised through the prophets and the scriptures; faith, to trust in your power to save; forgiveness, to renew our spirits and uphold us when we succumb to sin and our oppression.

ALL: Pour out your Spirit upon us, Holy Sovereign, Jesus, Christ, and strengthen us with these gifts.

LEADER: Our gay and gracious God, where shall we find your gay and lesbian saints? Have they all been lost to us? Bring us Saint Perpetua and Saint Felicitas, martyred women whose love and faith sustained generations of Christian hope. Bring us Saint Sergio and Saint Bacchus, whose fidelity and endurance inspired centuries of gay lovers. Bring us Saint Anselm, Saint Aelred, Saint Paulinus, and the nuns of Tegernsee, who revealed lesbian and gay love and courage to the church and the world so long ago.

(*Here the group may add more names memorable to the specific community.*)

ALL: Praise God for these valiant souls!

LEADER: Compassionate Spirit of God, unite us with the lives and visions of lesbian and gay heroes of our time. Unite us with . . . [*Here the congregation may give names and brief descriptions of contemporary people who are important to the specific community.*] Unite us with all the souls living and dead, especially those souls taken by violence and AIDS. Unite us with all who boldly pioneered a way of pride and justice.

ALL: Blessed Jesus, hold them to you closely and guide us in their footsteps.

LEADER: For all your silent, invisible, tireless workers—in our church, in homes throughout the world, everywhere your Spirit has gathered gay and lesbian people together, our prayers of thanksgiving and safety rise before you, that your saving, liberating Word may whisper to the heart of every person and that every soul may be freed from the hateful curse of oppression.

ALL: For all your saints, Sovereign God, we pray blessings and courage.

LEADER: Who are these lesbian and gay saints whom God loves and liberates? Where shall we find them?

ALL: We are all around you; we are here; and we praise and thank God for ourselves and each other.

LEADER: Bless us, all your saints, God of our birth. As we gather in your holy presence, unite us in all our glorious diversity to work your will in all the world; through Jesus Christ, who lives and reigns with you and the Holy Spirit, one God, now and forever.

ALL: Amen.

A CELEBRATION OF LESBIAN AND GAY PRIDE

Michael S. Piazza, Carol A. West, and *Paul A. Tucker*

Prelude

Concerns of the Congregation

Exchange of Peace

Call to Worship

ONE: God is merciful and gracious, slow to anger, and abounding in steadfast love.

ALL: We have gathered to hear the story of God and God's people.

ONE: It is a story of God's mercy and faithfulness.

ALL: It is our story, for we are God's people.

Processional Hymn

Collect

ALL: Once we were not a people at all, but now we are God's people. For that gift, O God, we thank you. Although others may say differently, help us never to forget that you, O God, are with us, for we are your gentle, angry, loving people. Amen.

Musical Offering

We Remember the Pain

ONE: Gay and lesbian people have survived thousands of years of brutality and persecution. We have been hunted, burned, tortured, excommunicated, killed, and labeled as heretics, sinners, and demon-possessed.

ALL: Still we have survived. How is that possible?

ONE: We survive because we share a common story and we gain strength from sharing that story. One generation tells the next. We cannot be destroyed unless they make us forget who we are.

ALL: Then let us not forget. Let us tell our stories and not leave out a line. Let us tell even the painful parts.

ONE: Lesbian and gay people have existed in every time and place. Let us remember with pride our story, even the tragic and painful parts. Weep if you must, but never forget.

Lighting of the First Candle of Pain
(*The World in Which We Live*)

ONE: We light this first candle of pain to remind us of the fear we experience in the world in which we live.

ALL: May the Light of Christ dispel all our fears.

Lighting of the Second Candle of Pain
(*Violence toward Our Community*)

ONE: Let us remember all those who have been victims of violence because of who they are.

ALL: May the Light of Christ bring peace to the world.

Lighting of the Third Candle of Pain
(*AIDS*)

ONE: Let us remember those who have died of AIDS, those who live with AIDS, and those who fear AIDS.

ALL: May the Light of Christ heal us of our diseases and remove our fear.

Lighting of the Fourth Candle of Pain
(*Internalized Homophobia*)

ONE: Let us remember all the ways that we as gay and lesbian people remain caught in our inner struggles.

ALL: May the Light of Christ break all the chains that bind us.

Hymn of Pain

"Singing for Our Lives" by Holly Near
(*Use first verse only.*)

We Remember Our Hope

ONE: Like the stories of others who have known the sting of oppression, our story is filled with pain and sorrow. We cannot pretend that it is otherwise.

ALL: But that is not our whole story. Let us celebrate our victories and our heroes, too.

ONE: They are really two sides of the same story. Sometimes it takes a tragedy to make us recognize our heroes. Sometimes it is only in the midst of pain that we can see there is hope.

ALL: We believe that evil cannot prevent God's promises from being fulfilled. Therefore the light of our hope grows stronger as we hold firm in our faith in Jesus Christ and in each other.

Lighting of the First Candle of Hope
(*Relationships*)

ONE: Let us remember the courage of those who express their love in courage and pride.

ALL: May the love in our lives shine through for all to see.

Lighting of the Second Candle of Hope
(*Heterosexual Heroes*)

ONE: Let us remember all those who are not gay or lesbian, but who share our struggle for justice and hope.

ALL: May our arms be open in our journey to embrace all who come in peace.

Lighting of the Third Candle of Hope
(*Gays and Lesbians of Faith*)

ONE: Let us remember people of faith who made it possible for us to be lesbian or gay and also people of faith.

ALL: We celebrate the great love of God for us and those who helped us know that love.

Lighting of the Fourth Candle of Hope
(*Gay and Lesbian Heroes*)

ONE: Let us remember those who by the courageous way they lead their lives are our heroes today.

ALL: Let us follow their example and leave a brighter way for those who follow us.

Hymn of Hope

"Singing for Our Lives" by Holly Near
(*Use verses 2 through 4.*)

Gospel Lesson

Sermon

Offering

Holy Communion

Prayer of Thanksgiving

Recessional Hymn

The Sending Forth

ONE: We have remembered our story, and much of it is sad.

ALL: But that is not the whole story, for we are not without hope. Our story is funny and happy, too.

ONE: We are fortunate, today, to be able to gather as a people of the church; as men and women; as lesbian and gay and bisexual and straight; as people of many origins and backgrounds.

ALL: We gather as a community with a common task of seeking justice, of living in shalom, of prophesying to the church and to the many communities that our lives touch. We are teachers, prophets, healers, interpreters, and lovers of life.

ONE: We all are called, as members of this community, to offer our gifts to the common journey. Our gifts are diverse and unique and cannot be replaced. Today, we affirm our loving acceptance of one another with all our varied gifts.

ALL: From the God within us, we affirm our love ministries. We smile in joyful acceptance of our loves, our lives, and our gifts. We are different: not queer, just special.

ONE: O God, who is our mother, father, friend, and lover, send us out from this place knowing in our hearts that we are your people and that no one can take that gift from us.

ALL: We go with sadness, laughter, joy, and hopefulness from this time of remembering.

ONE: For us and all oppressed people, this is our hope:

ALL: Next year, may all be free!

Benediction

Postlude

A RITE OF COMMISSIONING FOR
LESBIAN/GAY PRIDE CELEBRATIONS

D. B. Gregory Flaherty

This rite is designed to be used at the start of a lesbian/gay pride celebration such as a parade or festival. Christians may gather with the banner of the community, the cross, a pole with rainbow streamers, or some other identifying symbol. Water should be available for this rite.

OFFICIANT: Let us praise our Creator, Redeemer, and Sanctifier, Mother and Father God.

ALL: Amen.

OFFICIANT: Lord God, you created us in a bright array of color and diversity as people of your name. We come together to celebrate one of those many colors in our lives—the gift of homosexuality. We gather today with many others of our present and of our past. There are many who for different reasons are not here. We remember those who have died from AIDS, whose loving memories we carry with us today.

(*Names may be spoken aloud.*)

We remember those who lost their lives to hate crimes and other violence, whose loving memories we carry with us today.

(*Names may be spoken aloud.*)

We remember those who cannot be with us because of distance, because of current illness, or because of fear.

(*Names may be spoken aloud.*)

We remember and give praise for the lives and memories of these loved ones and revel in their living still in our midst.

(*Intercessions may be added for elected officials, church leaders, a spirit of understanding, and a commitment to justice; for the community, the sick, and for those who cannot participate in such a celebration due to fear and ignorance. The Lord's Prayer is then prayed, and a sign of peace is shared with all. A prayer of blessing, including a generous sprinkling of the assembly with water, concludes the rite.*)

OFFICIANT: God of the dance, we come before you this day to celebrate those whose daring moves have made a day like this possible. We practice our own steps, sometimes radical and laughed at, in hope that we will pave a route for tomorrow's dancers. Bless our time here today, our spirit of joy, our sign of pride; and give us many days to come in your love as we march toward your kingdom.

ALL: Amen.

OFFICIANT: Let us go forth in peace.

ALL: Thanks be to God.

CHRISTIAN AFFIRMATIONS OF LESBIANS AND GAY MEN: A SERVICE IN THE TAIZÉ STYLE

Kittredge Cherry and *Nathan Meckley*

An effective format for spiritual celebration of lesbian and gay pride originated with an ecumenical community in Taizé, France. The Taizé community was founded during World War II as a place of reconciliation by one known as Brother Roger. He and the first brothers provided refuge for resistance workers and refugees, especially Jews, and also offered hospitality to German prisoners in anti-Nazi France. Taizé has become an international point of pilgrimage, drawing tens of thousands of visitors every year from all over the world.

A style of singing and praying evolved in Taizé to facilitate worship by people who do not speak a common language. The service is simple and peaceful. Brief readings are done in a variety of languages. Generous periods of silence provide the opportunity for personal contemplative prayer. The simple musical themes and phrases are easily learned and tend to stay with the singer long after the sound has actually ceased, so the music is both popular and contemplative. There is no specified end to the music and the phrases may be repeated as long as desired, leading worshipers to achieve an internal quiet. The silence is as important as the songs and spoken prayer. In this way Taizé worship is like music: The silent rests are as important in creating beauty as are the sounds of sustained pitches.

Because lesbian and gay people have been excluded from so much of church life, the hope offered by Taizé's history of reconciliation, ecumenism, and internationalism is important for our community. Moreover, lesbian/gay spirituality liberates people to listen to God directly instead of letting only outside "authorities" define God's will; Taizé-style worship has the same effect.

In creating Taizé-style worship, let simplicity be the guiding principle. We usually place a cross and candles on the altar. Depending on the needs and desires of the local congregation, it may be appropriate to use icons. In leading worship, move with ease and serenity. Speak clearly, but say as little as possible. Musical performance should also be simple. Although there are no "star performers," we encourage the use of vocal and instrumental ensembles. When introducing each chant, emphasize the melody. An individual or ensemble may sing along to encourage congregational singing. Repeat each chant for several minutes, guided by the spiritual momentum of the congregation.

Resources for Taizé music and additional background information include *Music from Taizé* (Volumes I [1981] and II [1984]), *Cantos de Taizé* (1986), *Songs and Prayers from Taizé* (1991). The four volumes are available in basic (vocal), instrumental, and people's editions from G.I.A. Publications, Inc., 7404 S. Mason Ave., Chicago, IL 60638. Another valuable resource for Taizé worship is *Canticles and Gathering Prayers* by John P. Mossi and Suzanne Toolan, published in 1989 by St. Mary's Press, Winona, MN 55987. With one exception, all the music in this service can be found in these books. The last chant, "Singing for Our Lives," a song by Holly Near that has become the anthem of lesbian/gay liberation, is available from Redwood Cultural Work, P.O. Box 10408, Oakland, CA 94610. Other works by Near mentioned here can also be obtained from this source.

The theme of this service is Christian affirmations of lesbians and gay men. By changing the readings and music, the same format can be used for an unlimited variety of themes. When we followed this order of worship in the monthly Taizé service at Metropolitan Community Church of Los Angeles, we did all readings in both Spanish and English, but the languages can be varied based on the needs of the particular congregation. We often use only Bible readings because it is easier to find translations, but the service is enlivened when contemporary spiritual readings are included, as is the case in this particular service. Although there is no specified end for each song, we find this service format generally lasts about one hour.

Opening Chant

"Laudate Dominum," in *Music from Taizé* (vol. I)

Welcome

Scripture Reading with Response

As we hear readings from scripture, we will respond after each reading by singing.
(*Play and sing the response, in this case, "Arise, let your glory shine forth."*)
2 Samuel 1:17–18, 25–26

Ruth 1:8–9, 16–18
Isaiah 54:1; 56:4–5
Matthew 19:11–12

Silent Meditation

(*This should last about five minutes.*)

Chant

"Ubi Caritas," in *Music from Taizé* (vol. I)

Lesson

READER: To deal with the theme of homosexuality from a Christian perspective would seem to be a grand adventure.

That is the first thought that comes quickly to mind in response to the question, "Can I be a Christian person and a homosexual at the same time?" The question arises because for such a long time the majority of religious denominations said it was unthinkable to be both Christian and homosexual; it was an insanity and an immorality, a lack of respect for the doctrine of the institutional church.

I will try to express my point of view as Christian and homosexual at the same time. And for me, that is how it is: completely compatible. I believe in a God who is love, a God who is a fountain of infinite mercy, a God who calls us through to pure love. God doesn't ask for last names or ethnic or cultural background. God simply calls.

For me, service to God signifies joy because this same God has conducted me through the most beautiful process of interior liberation. I only wish to manifest the joy of serving a God who invites me to live an abundant life, a God who takes my whole life, not just a part of my life.

(This was written by the Reverend José Gonzalez, Latin Ministry Coordinator, Metropolitan Community Church of Los Angeles, California.)

Silent Meditation

(*This should last seven to ten minutes.*)

Chant

"O God, Hear My Prayer," in *Music from Taizé* (vol. II)

Community Prayer with Response

LEADER: For our time of community prayer, we invite you to offer aloud a brief phrase or sentence of prayer, after which we will sing, "God have mercy," "Kyrie eleison," in *Music from Taizé* (vol. I).

(NOTE: *There are several settings of "Kyrie eleison" of which any one may be chosen.*)

Chant

"Stay with Me," in *Music from Taizé* (vol. II)

Invitation to the Altar

LEADER: Jesus promised, "Come to me, all ye who labor and are heavy laden, and I will give you rest." As we sing the next three chants, you are invited to come to the altar in prayer and lay your burdens at the cross, to receive the rest and renewal that God offers, so you may go from here and walk in God's ways. Feel free to pray in whatever way is most comfortable, whether it is kneeling or standing at the altar or remaining in your seat.

Chants

"Nada Te Turbe," "Confitemini Domino," "Lamb of God," and "Singing for Our Lives"

(*As the Spirit moves during the last chant, the worship leader may want to urge the congregation to stand, join hands, and form a circle.*)

(Sources of chants suggested above are as follows: "Nada Te Turbe" is in *Cantos de Taizé*, Vol. I. "Confitemini Domino" is in *Music from Taizé*, Vol. II. "Agnus Dei" is from "Yesterday, Today and Forever," Communion Setting by Suzanne Toolan, 1987; copyright © 1988 G.I.A. Publications, Chicago, IL 60638. "Singing for Our Lives" by Holly Near is available from Redwood Cultural Work, P.O. Box 10408, Oakland, CA 94610.)

LITANY OF JUSTICE

Colleen Darraugh

This litany was written for the 1993 General Conference of the Universal Fellowship of Metropolitan Community Churches and was read on the day of President Bill Clinton's "Don't ask; don't tell" announcement concerning the presence of lesbians and gay men in the United States military. Encourage individuals to add or change items to reflect current justice issues.

The litany is written for four voices. Try to select people who reflect the widest diversity of your community. Print the congregational response in a number of languages to help people recognize that English is not the first language of all people and that justice issues are global issues. In preparing this rite, seek the help of members of the community who may know different languages to add to the following list:

I saw a new heaven and a new earth, for the former things had passed away. (*English*)

Je vis un ciel nouveau et une terre nouvelle, car les premiers ont disparu. (*French*)

Ich sah einen neuen Himmel und eine neue Erde; denn das Erste war vergangen. (*German*)

Ví un cielo nuevo y una tierra nueva; porque lo primero ya pasó. (*Spanish*)

VOICE 1: Would you please join us in the litany for justice by responding in whatever language is comfortable for you. At the end of each petition, the reader will say, "Oh, how we long for that new day!" Then you will respond as printed, or in another language of choice.

VOICE 2: Scripture urges us to love mercy, do justice, and walk humbly with our God. What would our world look like if we all truly worked for justice? Oh, how we long for that new day!

ALL: I saw a new heaven and a new earth, for the former things had passed away.

VOICE 3: The issues are complex but, God, we ask for justice, peace, and understanding in our world. God, we pray for an end to the fighting in Bosnia, Somalia, the Mid-East, and so many other places in our world. Oh, how we long for that new day!

ALL: I saw a new heaven and a new earth, for the former things had passed away.

VOICE 4: There are many in our world who thirst today. In many places in our world, there is not enough water, and in other places the water is polluted and unsafe to drink, including places under siege of flooding waters. God, may there be healing, safe waters for all. Oh, how we long for that new day!

ALL: I saw a new heaven and a new earth, for the former things had passed away.

VOICE 1: Racial strife is still present in our world. For the peoples of South Africa, we pray. For all those who are discriminated against because of the color of their skin, we pray. For all people to see and acknowledge race, color, and culture and to acknowledge that all are created in the image of God, we pray. What a day it will be when people can truly respect each other, and can live and work together in peace! Oh, how we long for that new day!

ALL: I saw a new heaven and a new earth, for the former things had passed away.

VOICE 2: We give thanks for those places in the world that have made progress in granting full human and civil rights to gay, lesbian, bisexual, and transgendered peoples. We give thanks for countries like Canada, Australia, Russia, and Israel, who have lifted the ban on gays and lesbians in their military. Oh, how we long for that new day!

ALL: I saw a new heaven and a new earth, for the former things had passed away.

VOICE 3: We pray for the United States of America, for President Clinton, and for all gay, lesbian, bisexual, and transgendered people who are serving or wish to serve in the military. It is said that peace is not the absence of conflict but the presence of justice. Today, we express our anger at the absence of justice in the compromise of "Don't ask; don't tell" given for gays and lesbians serving in the U. S. military. Oh, how we long for that new day!

ALL: I saw a new heaven and a new earth, for the former things had passed away.

VOICE 4: Our brothers and sisters in Argentina and many other countries live with a constant threat against their lives because of who they are and whom they love. We pray for their safety, for their courage, and for justice in their land. Oh, how we long for that new day!

ALL: I saw a new heaven and a new earth, for the former things had passed away.

VOICE 1: For the refugees and homeless of our world, we pray. Oh, how we long for that new day!

ALL: I saw a new heaven and a new earth, for the former things had passed away.

VOICE 2: For the malnourished and starving of our world, we pray. Oh, how we long for that new day!

ALL: I saw a new heaven and a new earth, for the former things had passed away.

VOICE 3: For global economics and a sharing of the world's resources, we pray. Oh, how we long for that new day!

ALL: I saw a new heaven and a new earth, for the former things had passed away.

VOICE 4: For the planet, the environment, and justice for all God's creation, we pray. Oh, how we long for that new day!

ALL: I saw a new heaven and a new earth, for the former things had passed away.

ALL FOUR VOICES: God has promised us a new day of justice for all, a day of Jubilee. But it takes all of us working with God, loving mercy, doing justice, and living humbly with our God. Together let us commit to working for that new day when all shall say:

ALL: I saw a new heaven and a new earth, for the former things had passed away!

LITANY FOR DIVINE INTERVENTION

James Lancaster

This liturgy is a ritual of empowerment for gay/lesbian communities who find themselves under attack by particular political or religious groups or individuals. It is a ritual to express and channel justifiable anger and outrage, and to plead for divine intervention in combating falsehoods and heterosexist myths being used to oppress God's lesbian and gay people. It is a way to draw the community together and inspire strength and confidence in God's promises of deliverance. The present liturgy is inspired by the rite of greater excommunication in the *Pontificale Romanum,* the old Roman Catholic rite. Historically, it was used to suppress so-called enemies of the church and false teachings. This is an attempt to transform it from a symbol of oppression into a life-giving ritual for our times.

This ritual is not a judgment on the souls of persons or members of subject groups. The status of individual souls before God is not subject to speculation. Only the earthly conduct, speech, and writings of any person should be condemned. Salvation, after all, is extended to all people, even to oppressors.

People or organizations who are the subject of this petition should be chosen with great care and deliberation. They should be highly visible figures or organizations who habitually and relentlessly oppress and seek to deny the rights and humanity of lesbian/gay people, women, people of color, persons with AIDS, and the like. I caution against using it for local figures or persons who oppose a certain agenda on a single issue; a simple prayer service should suffice for smaller matters. Such would reduce the ritual to silly and petty politicking and the participants to the level of medieval popes. Specificity is important: A white supremacist organization would be appropriate, but to invoke it against "all hate groups" or "anyone who ever hated anyone" would obviously weaken the power and particularity of this ritual and render meaningless the pleas for God to stop certain oppressive acts and restore grace and redemption to the souls committing these acts.

A detailed and far-ranging list of the reasons that a person or group is singled out should be compiled to be read during the ceremony; a laundry list of names would lessen the impact of the ceremony, and the congregation must understand what is happening at the time, and why it happens.

Parenthetical instructions are given in italics. The lessons are suggestions only. A dropcloth is recommended to protect the floor or carpet before the altar. Dim light, at least in the altar area, is preferable.

MINISTER: God be with you.

CONGREGATION: And also with you.

MINISTER: Let us pray. We glorify and affirm, holy and eternal God, your power to save, your strength to redeem. Fill us with the sweet water of forgiveness to slake our bitter thirst for vengeance. Hear in these words the earnest pleas of your children for protection. Amen.

Lesson

Leviticus 26:[27–40], 41–46

Psalm

139 (*Sung or recited responsively; the entire psalm is recommended.*)

Lesson

2 Peter 2:10–14
Luke 17:1–4

Homily

(*Minister should spend a little time preparing congregation for the ceremony, telling what it signifies and what it does not. At the conclusion of the homily a hymn may be sung. A group of assisting ministers, preferably twelve, or perhaps one for each subject of the ritual, gather before the altar with candles, facing the congregation. Two acolytes light the candles, then take their places at the ends of the altar, facing it. Each should have a bell before them at the end of the altar. The presiding minister then stands in the middle of the twelve or before them, holding open the book in which the subjects and their condemned acts are listed, and addresses the congregation.*)

MINISTER: God be with you.

CONGREGATION: And also with you.

MINISTER: Open your hearts.

CONGREGATION: We open them to God.

MINISTER: Let us thank God.

CONGREGATION: It is right to give God thanks and praise.

MINISTER: Holy God, Mighty One, who judges the nations and protects the innocent, great are your wonders and mysterious your ways. We bring before you brothers and sisters of our own flesh who have sinned against us. Their wicked acts burn before us like the fire that does not go out. Hear our petitions, which we offer in humility, mindful of your slow patience and quick mercy. Take these brothers and sisters under your wings, that their evil will no longer hurt your people.

CONGREGATION: God, save us from our enemies.

MINISTER: Hear, O God, the ways of the wicked and the sins of the unjust: N., who . . . .

CONGREGATION: God, save us from our enemies.

(*Repeat for each person's or group's name and deeds, followed by congregational response.*)

MINISTER (*after all the names have been read, holding book open and repeating the names*): N., this congregation of God's faithful people declares you to be in danger of God's wrath. May your spiteful words be swallowed up in insensible noise, never to harm or incite violence against our people.

CONGREGATION: God, save us from our enemies.

MINISTER: Let your hateful deeds be shrouded in fog so that no one may see or know them.

CONGREGATION: God, save us from our enemies.

MINISTER: May all your plotting come to naught, and your wicked thoughts against us be thrown into confusion and never find expression.

CONGREGATION: God, save us from our enemies.

MINISTER: Let your writings be gibberish to all who read them.

CONGREGATION: God, save us from our enemies.

MINISTER: May God not hear your prayers until they are prayers of repentance and pleas for forgiveness.

CONGREGATION: God, save us from our enemies.

MINISTER: As Jesus cleared the Temple of thieves and charlatans who preyed on the faithful, so let God clear Christianity of your lies, which seek to rob us of our dignity.

CONGREGATION: God, save us from our enemies.

MINISTER: May the blighted light of your malicious words and injurious deeds be hidden away from all God's people and concealed beneath God's hand. Let there be no harm, no hurt, in all God's holy mountain: Until the time of your repentance, may your evil intentions be swallowed up in darkness!

(*Minister shuts book heavily, loudly, as all lights are turned off. Acolytes begin ringing bells and assisting ministers to dash their candles to the ground.* [*Alternatively, candles may be extinguished in a basin of water.*] *Silence for a period.*)

MINISTER (*as bright lights fill the sanctuary*): Let us pray. Life-saving and life-giving God, we beseech you for the redemption of these men and women, that your miracle of love may free them from the shackles of hate; that trust in you may replace fear of others; that their destructive words, thoughts, and deeds may be forgotten and in their place be brought forth bright visions of peace, unity, justice, and joyous humanity. We pray for the repentance of these brothers and sisters, that they may harm no one ever again, and that you may gather them up passionately as what was lost but is now found. Then we will gladly welcome them beside us at the great and promised feast.

CONGREGATION: Come, Sovereign Jesus. Amen.

MINISTER (*addressing people*): Be vigilant, be watchful, for there are those who prowl like lions in the night, seeking whom they may devour. Trust in God and in the goodness of love, that salvation may flow upon all the people of God.

(*If worship is concluded, end with this dismissal; if worship service continues, a hymn may be sung.*)

MINISTER: Go in peace, serve God.
CONGREGATION: Thanks be to God.

A SERVICE OF WORSHIP FOR EMPOWERMENT

Lindsay Louise Biddle, editor

The following service was celebrated in more than fifty communities across the Presbyterian Church (U.S.A.) in solidarity with the commissioning as evangelist of the Reverend Dr. Jane Adams Spahr by the Downtown United Presbyterian Church in Rochester, New York, on March 6, 1993.

Along with the text for the service, these churches were sent a triangular piece of fabric, which they were asked to display during the service, for example, pinned to a parament or hung from a cross or a candlestick. They were also asked to provide pencils and paper for people to write their statements of commitment during the service. The triangles and statements from all the services were gathered by Presbyterians for Lesbian and Gay Concerns for use during the Presbyterian General Assembly. The triangles were sewn together and used in worship; the statements were balled up and put into a large container to be shaken at the General Assembly as a symbol of their efforts to "shake up" the church.

This liturgy was a collaborative effort that included heterosexual, gay, lesbian, and bisexual persons, all committed to ensuring the full participation of all people in the church regardless of sexual orientation. Contributors include Chris Glaser, Howard Warren, Jane Spahr, Margee Adams Iddings, David Romig, Lisa Larges, Jim Beates, Gail Ricciuti, Susan Kramer, Coni Staff, Barry Smith, and Lindsay Biddle.

Call to Worship

(*This may be spoken responsively among all and multiple voices in the congregation, among all and the left and right sides of the congregation, or between all and a leader. All and Leader are used here for simplicity.*)

ALL: God calls us, amid our anger and frustration, to celebrate the ministry of all people, especially lesbian, gay, bisexual, and transgendered people, and to recommit ourselves to the church's struggle for justice-love, inclusiveness, and more light.

LEADER: Some of us gather in parts of the world that protect the civil rights of all citizens regardless of sexual orientation.

ALL: Some of us gather in places that do not have laws forbidding violence, harassment, and discrimination toward lesbian, gay, bisexual, and transgendered individuals, couples, and their families.

LEADER: Some of us gather in congregations that publicly welcome all persons who profess faith in Jesus Christ, renounce evil and affirm reliance on God's grace, and intend to participate actively and responsibly in the worship and mission of the church.

ALL: Some of us are not free to tell other members of our churches that we are here today.

LEADER: Some of us gather in areas of the church that are on the cutting edge of reform and renewal.

ALL: Some of us gather in modern catacombs, by word of mouth, in the deep undercurrents of our church that effect change person by person.

LEADER: If one of us suffers, we all suffer. If one of us is honored, we all rejoice together.

ALL: Out of our suffering, let us worship our Creator, who made each one of us different and named all of us "very good." Let us praise the Spirit of God, who gives to each of us varieties of gifts for the common good. Let us honor the body of Christ, who calls us to love and to care for one another.

Hymn

(*Tune: Lancashire, "Lead On, O King Eternal," with new words by Chris Glaser, © Chris R. Glaser*)

Lead on, O sacred Spirit, your soul we now behold,
In love and flesh and visions, of those "outside" the fold,
The cornerstones rejected, the children cast away,
And precious pearls downtrodden: bi, lesbian, and gay.

Lead on, O sacred Spirit, beyond religion's chains
Of laws that bind our spirits, and thwart your sov'reign reign.
Deliver us to worship, you on your hallowed cross;
Free us to preach your gospel, and count the church as loss.

Lead on, O sacred Spirit, in our ordained search
That takes us from the closet, our grave within the church:
The quest to choose life, to love with all your heart,
The call to touch with healing, your body torn apart.

Prayer of Confession

O wildly inclusive God, who loves all of the beautiful rainbow of human sexual orientation, remind us that we have a very practical Trinity—one who gives life, one who redeems life, one who stays with us forever. Hear our groans, Holy Spirit, particularly to make a home in all churches that call themselves the body of Christ: for bisexuals, gay men, heterosexuals, lesbian women, and transgendered persons. At times we are overwhelmed and hurt by this angry exclusion. At these times let us realize how much more hurt you are. (*Pause for silent prayer.*) Come, Holy Spirit, come! Free your people! Alleluia! Amen.

Declaration of Acceptance

Romans 8:28

Response to Being Accepted

Romans 8:38–39

Prayer for Illumination

Spirit of the One and the Many, you who live in us and through us: We feel so connected in this intertwining. We feel alive in your and our passion. We feel heard and affirmed by your and our love. You who whisper in the deepest parts of us, still us into a peace we dare to imagine. Center us in you—in us—to break free. Peace and passion us into liberation. Then let us soar with you, yet be grounded in us, in the healing of the earth, in the healing of each other. Amen.

Scripture

Luke 13:10–17

Interpretation of the Word

Hymn

(*Tune: St. Denio, "Immortal, Invisible," with new words by Margee Adams Iddings*)

> O God, hear our cry from the depth of our pain.
> We long for your justice and mercy to reign.
> Come gather our anger, frustration, and rage
> And make them constructive in the dawning age.

When one is excluded, the whole body hurts
And suffers an anguish that cannot give birth
To anything other than shock, grief, and fear.
We seek now your wisdom—a pathway made clear.

We know Christ intended that all be a part
Of that commonwealth where love was from the start
The measure of all that could ever be used
To test someone's worthiness. This test we choose.

To end this apartheid, we earnestly plea
For your tender passion—invade and set free.
May justice-love firmly be planted and fed
In each congregation, disciple—Christ led.

Affirmation of Faith

(*This may be spoken responsively among multiple voices in the congregation or between all and a leader. All and Leader are used here for simplicity.*)

ALL: At a crucial point in the life of the early church, some believers stood up and said:

LEADER: "It is necessary for the Gentiles to be circumcised and keep the law of Moses."

ALL: But Peter said, "Why are you putting God to the test by placing on the neck of the disciples a yoke that neither we nor our ancestors have been able to bear? We believe that we will be saved through the grace of the Lord Jesus, just as they will."

LEADER: Then the apostles and the elders, with the consent of the whole church, sent the following letter:

ALL: "It has seemed good to the Holy Spirit . . .

LEADER: and to us . . .

ALL: to impose on you no further burden than these essentials."

LEADER: Grace was to be mediated universally—to Gentile as to Jew— through all the new creation.

Prayers of the People

LEADER: Dear Holy Spirit,

ALL: Never has the church been in greater need of your revolutionary, radicalizing presence. You have moved across the globe and brought democracy and peace where we little expected it. You have moved across the nation and brought change and hope when we most needed it. As you have moved upon the body politic, we pray you will move upon the body of Christ, bringing new life to its withering appendages, especially our own Presbyterian Church (U.S.A.).

Inspire us with the anger of Jesus, clearing the Temple grounds, damning the self-righteous, silencing authorities, demanding the disciples' devotion, risking a cross to bring life. Inspire us with the joy of Pentecost, descending with flames of passion, opening our mouths, giving us language to speak, transforming pathos to triumph, converting strangers to faith. Inspire us with the gospel's vision of a new heaven and a new earth, of a common spiritual wealth, of an inclusive church, of truth written in our hearts, of justice embodied in our love.

On your altar we lay our anger and fury at the Presbyterian Church's denial of your call to lesbians, gay men, bisexuals, and transgendered persons. On your altar we lay the hope of martyrs: Janie, Lisa, Bill, Sandy, Bet, Diana, Scott, and countless more.
(*Pause for spoken or silent naming of others.*)
Their hope cries out for justice. How long, O Spirit? Hear these prayers, we pray in, with, and for you.

O God, give all who are afraid, who feel this to be a strange new world, the gift of truth, insight, and inescapable compassion toward lesbian, gay, bisexual, and transgendered neighbors; that we may walk hand in hand into the realm you have promised us and sit down together at the joyful feast that awaits us in your presence.

O God, give all lesbian, gay, bisexual, and transgendered persons strength to find, through you, the courage to be themselves and fulfill your purpose in life. Move us all beyond oppression, discrimination, isolation, and loneliness into a new hope and a new life of purpose, confidence, and responsibility.

O God, may our witness to the power of your healing hope and love so transform our church and our world that, everywhere, people with HIV/AIDS may know that all can go to the church for help and solace in time of need.

We pray for an end to the idolization of scripture and the prostitution of the word for our own purposes.
(*Pause for spoken or silent prayers.*)
O God, prepare our hearts and minds to be loved into doing

justice. Restore our bodies and souls to enjoy our sexualities and spiritualities and express them to your glory.

The Spirit who calls creation out of chaos, liberation out of bondage, justice out of oppression, serenity out of whirlwinds, blessing out of baptism, empowerment out of vulnerability, reformation out of turpitude—use us as seeds of change, as the leaven of transformation, and as vessels of your healing balm, while the church abandons its own calling to deny ours, wounding itself and others. Amen.

We Recommit Ourselves to God

ONE: The triangle made of fabric serves as a visual and tactile symbol of our brokenness and connectedness as a church. World War II concentration camp prisoners identified as homosexuals, the "third sex," were forced to wear the triangle. Like the cross, the triangle once symbolized oppression and now symbolizes liberation. Today we recommit ourselves to liberating our church to lesbian, gay, bisexual, and transgendered people everywhere.

Call to Recommitment

ALL: God with nimble fingers creates the substance for spinning threads, weaves those threads into pieces of fabric, and sews those pieces into larger, multicolored, diverse, bright and shining works of art. In our church, we are like scraps of material, torn apart yet of the same cloth. At this time, we join with others across our denomination to offer the pieces of ourselves to God and the people of God. May our lives be quilted together by God into one multicolored, diverse, bright and shining, beautiful tapestry.

(*At this time, each may recommit to God gifts of time, talent, solidarity, in the church's struggle for justice-love, inclusivity, and more light. On paper write your personal statement of recommitment, but do not sign your name. You are invited to bring your statement of recommitment forward as the congregation joins in the following hymn. Verses of "Singing for Our Lives" may be alternated with readings from official church statements on homosexuality.*)

Hymn

What follows is an adaptation of "Singing for Our Lives" by Holly Near. Copyright 1979 Hereford Music. This and other works by Holly Near are available from Redwood Cultural Work, P.O. Box 10408, Oakland, California 94610.

We are a gentle, angry people,
And we are singing, singing for our lives.
We are a gentle, angry people,
And we are singing, singing for our lives.

We are gay and straight together,
And we are singing, singing for our lives.
We are gay and straight together,
And we are singing, singing for our lives.

We are a many-colored rainbow,
And we are singing, singing for our lives.
We are a many-colored rainbow,
And we are singing, singing for our lives.

We are young and old together,
And we are singing, singing for our lives.
We are young and old together,
And we are singing, singing for our lives.

We are a diversely abled people,
And we are singing, singing for our lives.
We are a diversely abled people,
And we are singing, singing for our lives.

We are a wildly inclusive people,
And we are singing, singing for our lives.
We are a wildly inclusive people,
And we are singing, singing for our lives.

Prayer of Dedication

ALL: Spirit Wind, love us to justice. Hold us tight to your bosom until we know beyond words the goodness of our spirit while linked with yours. Then may we hold hands and stride together into the play and the work and the life that is ours to live with you. Keep spiriting your wind within us, and may we keep saying yes.

Hymn: "We Limit Not the Truth of God"

(*Tune: St. Anne, "O God, Our Help in Ages Past." Stanzas 1–2 were adapted by Barry Smith from a hymn by George Rawson (1807–1889) and are based on the words of Rev. John Robinson to the Pilgrims in 1620. Stanzas 3–5 are the original work of Barry Smith, 1985.)*

We limit not the truth of God
To our poor reach of mind,
By notions of our day and sect:
Crude, partial, and confined.

For God has yet more light and truth
To break forth from the Word;
So let a new and better hope
Within our hearts be stirred.

We pray for God's light in our world
Where war and pain exist,
And shadows often fill our hearts,
God's Word we still resist.

Yet God still gives more light, more truth,
More joy, more love, more peace;
God's Word within again burns bright,
Light shining without cease.

So let us work throughout the world,
God's children to unite,
Till peace and justice reign at last,
In endless days of light!

Benediction

WHAT IS CHURCH?

The Cathedral Project

This liturgy was created and celebrated as a street Mass on April 2, 1989, by the Cathedral Project, a coalition of disenfranchised Catholics. They initially gathered together in reaction to the 1987 expulsion of Dignity, a community of lesbian/gay Catholics, from the church where they met weekly.

According to Joanne Still, member and spokesperson, "The resulting group determined that our witness should take the form of liturgies which could transform the Mass into an action that was meaningful to us, and through which we could clearly demonstrate our presence as 'church.' ''

Processional: The Laying of the Wreath

LEADER: In the Middle Ages, the Song of Solomon was a favorite text, often used as an allegory of the relationship of Christ to the church and Christ's (lover/spouse) relationship with each of the faithful, continuing a Hebrew tradition of the celebration of God in the sensuality of lovemaking bodies. This morning we also continue that tradition. Our witness in St. Patrick's Cathedral has always been about our love.

The Song of Solomon is vivacious with love, a litany of seductive image, filled both with longing and satisfaction, where body and soul are indivisible in the experience of love and hence (we will add) indivisible in the experience of faith. The rejection of the love between gay men and between lesbian women by the church hierarchy is profoundly much more than a rejection of us, gay and lesbian people; it is a rejection of all sexuality. It is a rejection of the body itself. It is to reduce God to a desert without water.

The church hierarchy's persecution of gay and lesbian people is a denial and refusal of the experience of the human body as a participant in salvation, redemption, and God's justice. With our witness to our church, we do not seek to restore ourselves in good standing to the church, but rather we seek to restore for everyone and for all the church the jubilant recognition of the place of the loving and lovemaking human body in salvation and justice. When we live in the kingdom, we bring our full human presence, body and soul. Is this not the promise of the resurrection? And when we make love without fear and in freedom—wherever we have learned to love—respecting one another and caring for one another, we bring more of the kingdom into the world, even as we were commanded by Christ.

Reading

Song of Solomon 5:10–16

Song of the People Gathering

"The Rose"

Call to Worship

LEADER: When we gather, we gather as a people of faith, a people in love, and a people in witness to our love and faith. We also gather as church.

Yet those in the Roman Catholic Church hierarchy tell us that we are not the church, our love is not a love sanctioned by God, an event of the incarnation. However, we know the hierarchy is wrong. We must tell this to the people of God, whom, after all, Vatican II did declare to be the true church.

The hierarchy is wrong not only to deny our human identity of love but also to have rejected us and so many others. Because they have been so overweening to say they alone can speak for God, they are also wrong to call themselves church. Church does not exclude. Our church is catholic—it will include and nurture all love and all faith.

We know that faith is a risk, is a danger, is a leap toward God, trusting God's grace and using every part of our being. So today, we articulate that risk of faith and we ask ourselves, What is church?

Our readings today, our witness today, will ask that question again and again, from traditional church documents, from other texts, and of each other. Sometimes the question of what church is can be painful and the answering proposals negative or ambivalent. But we can accept that. The time we are in, like every other era in human history, requires obedience to faith, not to an institutional church, that we follow the movement of the Spirit and not be enslaved by orthodoxy or other idolatry.

In fact, our faith requires that we also risk ourselves in public action and that we assist God's will to redeem the church so that it might become a fitting sanctuary for the people of God, so it might indeed serve as a door to the kingdom.

So, today, as we gather in Christ, we have gathered as church, and we have gathered in joy.

Reading

"The Church-floore" by George Herbert

Song for Call to Worship

"Amazing Grace"

Opening Prayer

LEADER: We are asking and answering the question, "What is church?"
ONE: Church is . . . (*Here individuals offer their definitions of church as they feel moved. Each definition is affirmed by the response.*)
ALL: In obedience to the Spirit.

Song

"Freedom"

First Reading

LEADER: Our readings today will each be a dialogue. Questions or situations proposed by the first text of each reading will be responded to, directly or indirectly, by the second text. The first texts will be from the Old and New Testaments. The responding texts will be from our contemporaries, as we struggle today with questions of faith and witness.

Part 1: Psalm 94:3–9

Part 2: William, from the base community at Solentiname, Nicaragua, describes how the church formed among the people of God becomes the eyes and ears of God.

Song

"It Could Have Been Me"

Second Reading

Part 1: Ephesians 2:19–22

Part 2: Reading from pages 34–35 of the essay "Before I Had a Name for God," by Martha Courtot, in *A Faith of One's Own: Explorations by Catholic Lesbians,* edited by Barbara Zanotti (Trumansburg, N.Y.: Crossing Press, 1986).

Song

"Alleluia"

Gospel Reading and Response

Part 1: Mark 11:11–23

Part 2: (*Leader introduces a reading from James Baldwin's* The Fire Next Time *by saying:*) James Baldwin was a child preacher in Harlem in the 1930s. He came to understand, however, that his way to follow the light and to fulfill his own obligations of faith was to leave his church. A black, gay man, Baldwin's journey became instead to find the complex truth of people, his people, black people, gay people—all people. He believed that the current regime of Christianity distorted the significance and worth in the equality of all people, and had contributed, even, to racism and division among people. It became his work to find the proper words to correctly name his people, who had been so oppressed, as a way to heal his people, both in anger and in love, and, equally universally, to articulate relations of justice among all people. Is this not a faithful search for God? Do we not have, as gay and lesbian people, the same task for ourselves?

Song

"Choose Life"

Prayers of the Faithful

LEADER: If there is to be a justification for church continuing, an integrity to our gathering and a redemption for our tradition, then we must make it so, fully alive and committed in mind, body, heart, and soul. For our Prayers of the Faithful this morning, let us renew our vows to love and justice, our vows to our Lover, God.

(*Excerpted from Dignity/New York's Easter renewal of baptismal promises and profession of faith.*)

ALL: Because of our belief in God as creator,
    we choose to be a people
    who will not jeopardize creation
    by sanctioning nuclear power and weapons
    or by lending our support to any oppressor:
    grateful for our environment
    we will care for the land
    and see that water and air remain pure.
        Because of our belief in Jesus as redeemer,
    we choose to be a people of peace and nonviolence.
        Because of our belief in Jesus as redeemer,
    we choose to be a people
    who uproot the sources of violence and oppression
    within ourselves and our society.
        Because of our belief in Jesus as redeemer
    we choose to commit ourselves
    to change our lives in simplicity and responsibility
    so that others may live.
        Because of our belief in God as spirit,

we choose to respect and appreciate
all persons whose religious expression
and understanding differ from ours.
   Because of our belief in God as spirit,
we choose to affirm and encourage
the prophetic voices
that recognize both the sin and the need of our times.
We believe that the gift of the Spirit
challenges us to a new vision
of what the world can be,
calling us
to go beyond established social, political,
and religious structures
to create a new world
in the spirit of the gospel of Jesus.
   Because of our belief in God the creator,
Jesus the redeemer,
and the Holy Spirit, the sanctifier,
we affirm that all human beings,
as spiritual beings in flesh,
receive from God the gift of their sexuality
that through it, they may express their love
and grow in love for one another,
achieving their sanctification in love.
   We believe that gay and lesbian persons are members of Christ,
numbered among the people of God;
that we have an inherent dignity because
God created us,
Christ died and rose for us,
and the Holy Spirit sanctified us.
   We believe that gay and lesbian persons can express their sexuality
physically in a unitive manner
that is loving,
life-giving,
life-affirming,
redeeming,
and sanctifying.
   Because of our belief in the church as community,
we choose to have no superiors or inferiors among us.

We affirm the dignity and giftedness of women.
We commit ourselves to a prayer
whose language includes women and men equally.
    Because of our belief in church as community,
we commit ourselves to grow in faithfulness to God,
and to one another,
and to the whole human family.
    We commit ourselves to living out
this vision of the church,
regardless of what it may cost.

Preparation of the Gifts and Song

Eucharistic Prayer

The Lord's Prayer

(*Recite the traditional prayer and sing a song of your choice.*)

Kiss of Peace

Breaking of Bread

Songs

"Agnus Dei" and "Let Us Break Bread Together"

Concluding Prayer and Benediction

Song

"Good News"

A PRAYER

Malcolm Boyd

Christ, as lesbians and gay men we stand inside your church and know a wholeness that can benefit it. We learned long ago that we must regard the lilies of the field, putting our trust in you.

Pressured to hide our identities and gifts, we have served you with an unyielding, fierce, vulnerable love inside the same church that condemned us.

Carefully taught that we must feel self-loathing, nevertheless we learned integrity and dignity and how to look into your face and laugh with grateful joy, Jesus.

Although we have suffered a long and continuing torture, we assert a stubborn, unshakeable faith in your holy justice.

Negativism was drummed into us as thoroughly as if we were sheet metal. We learned what it is to be misunderstood, perceived as alien, even sometimes hated. Yet, because of your grace and love, we witness to the fullness and beauty of all human creation, including ours, in your image.

We are alive and well and stand inside your church. Bless us, Christ, to your service.

Contributors

The Reverend Dr. Marilyn McCord Adams was ordained a priest in 1987 at Trinity Episcopal Church, Los Angeles, where she enjoyed a ministry among lesbian and gay persons. After twenty-one years in the philosophy department at UCLA, she is now professor of historical theology at Yale Divinity School and the Department of Religious Studies at Yale.

The Reverend Lindsay Louise Biddle of Minneapolis is one of many Presbyterians for Lesbian and Gay Concerns. She is a member of the Twin Cities Area Presbytery and pastors a congregation.

The Reverend Malcolm Boyd, Episcopal priest/activist/author, has written twenty-five books, including *Gay Priest, Take Off the Masks*, and the spiritual classic *Are You Running with Me, Jesus?* He is chaplain of AIDS ministries of the Episcopal Diocese of Los Angeles, and serves on the staff of St. Augustine-by-the-Sea Episcopal Church in Santa Monica. He recently celebrated his seventieth birthday and lives in Los Angeles with his life partner, Mark Thompson, author of *Gay Spirit* and senior editor of *The Advocate*.

Kevin Calegari was president of Dignity/USA from 1991 to 1993. A student at the Graduate Theological Union in Berkeley, California, he and his partner, Tom Kaun, have been together for more than ten years.

The Reverend Steve Carson is ordained in the Universal Fellowship of Metropolitan Community Churches. He received his Master of Divinity degree from Union Theological Seminary, New York, and has served Metropolitan Community Churches in New York, Boston, and San Francisco.

The Cathedral Project grew out of the witness of a group of gay men from Dignity/New York who, in 1987, following the banning of Dignity from its place of weekly worship, refused to become invisible. On the first Sunday of each month, these men and their supporters regularly attended mass at St. Patrick's Cathedral. During John Cardinal O'Connor's homily, the men would stand in silent prayer and witness. One month, as protestors stood silently during the homily, New York police swarmed through the sanctuary and down the pews. Those who stood were arrested and taken to the local precinct in paddy wagons. Among them was Charles Frederick, whose organizational ability brought the Cathedral Project into existence. In response to the arrests, Dignity/New York issued a call to the lesbian and gay community to join the organization in a re-formation of its public witness. This action was necessary because the "Trustees of the Cathedral" had obtained a legal injunction against members of Dignity/New York, and any persons who supported them, to keep them from entering the cathedral wearing buttons, armbands, or any other accessories that identified the wearer as lesbian or gay.

The Reverend Kittredge Cherry is an executive at the International Headquarters of the Universal Fellowship of Metropolitan Community Churches, where her responsibilities include communications and ecumenical relations. She represents UFMCC to the National Council of Churches (USA) and the World Council of Churches. A graduate of the University of Iowa, she studied in Japan on a Rotary International Journalism Scholarship and earned a Master of Divinity degree from the Pacific School of Religion, Berkeley, California. Cherry is the author of *Hide and Speak: How to Free Ourselves from Our Secrets* (HarperSanFrancisco, 1991) and *Womansword: What Japanese Words Say About Women* (Kodansha International, 1987). She lives in Los Angeles with her spouse, Audrey E. Lockwood, who is district manager of a financial consulting firm.

The Reverend Colleen Darraugh is senior pastor of Harvest Metropolitan Community Church, Denton, Texas. A native of Toronto, Canada, she graduated from Emmanuel College, Toronto School of Theology, and the University of Toronto. She received clergy credentials in UFMCC in 1986 and served as the liturgist for the UFMCC General Conference in 1993.

Dr. Elias Farajaje-Jonez is associate professor of the history of religions at Howard University School of Divinity, Washington, D.C. He is an Orthodox priest ordained by the Orthodox Church of France, but also practices the Yoruba and Native American religions. Dr. Farajaje-Jonez is of African and Cherokee descent and describes himself as "a queer-identified bisexual/two-spirit person." He chairs the political action committee of the District of Columbia Coalition of Black Lesbians, Gay Men, and Bisexuals.

D. B. Gregory Flaherty holds a master's degree in theology from St. Mary's University in Baltimore, Maryland. His interests have always included music and liturgics. He has worked with the New Ways Ministry, an organization promoting reconciliation and justice between lesbian and gay Catholics and the church, and the National Conference of Jewish and Christian Seminarians.

The Reverend Elder Darlene Garner celebrates herself as a woman of African, Cherokee, Mohawk, and Irish ancestry. She has served the Universal Fellowship of Metropolitan Community Churches in Philadelphia and Baltimore and is currently a pastor at Metropolitan Community Church of Northern Virginia. She was elected in 1993 as UFMCC's first African American elder. Baptized into the National Baptist Church at the age of seven, she went on to work as a legal secretary and Girl Scout executive before entering the ministry. She is a founding cochair of the National

Coalition of Black Lesbians and Gays. Reverend Garner is the mother of four children and has four grandchildren.

Chris Glaser, a resident of Atlanta, leads retreats and workshops throughout North America. He is the author of four books, most recently a 366-day devotional, *The Word Is Out: The Bible Reclaimed for Lesbians and Gay Men* (HarperSanFrancisco, 1994). He is also the author of *Uncommon Calling, Come Home!,* and *Coming Out to God* (Louisville, Ky.: Westminster/John Knox Press). He received his Master of Divinity degree from Yale Divinity School, and served on the Presbyterian Task Force to Study Homosexuality. For nearly ten years he was executive director of the Lazarus Project, a ministry of reconciliation between the church and the lesbian and gay community at the West Hollywood Presbyterian Church in Los Angeles.

The Reverend Dr. Carter Heyward, along with ten other women, was ordained "irregularly" into the Episcopal priesthood in 1974 before the Episcopal Church authorized the ordination of women. Five years later, she came out as a lesbian. Since 1975, she has been on the faculty of the Episcopal Divinity School, Cambridge, Massachusetts, where she is the Howard Chandler Robbins Professor of Theology. She is the author of numerous critically acclaimed articles and books, including *Touching Our Strength: The Erotic as Power and the Love of God* (HarperSanFrancisco, 1989) and *When Boundaries Betray Us: Beyond Illusions of What Is Ethical in Therapy and Life* (HarperSanFrancisco, 1993).

Thomas Kaun chairs the National Worship Committee of Dignity/USA. He is a librarian and lives in San Francisco with Kevin Calegari, his partner of more than ten years.

The Reverend Dr. Louis F. Kavar is field director for global outreach with the Universal Fellowship of Metropolitan Community Churches. Raised in the Byzantine Catholic Church, he holds a master's degree in spirituality from Duquesne University and a doctorate in counseling from the University of Pittsburgh. He has written four books, including *To Celebrate and to Mourn: Liturgical Resources for Worshiping Communities Living with AIDS* (1989).

James Lancaster is a writer living in Los Angeles. Raised in the Southern Baptist Church, he has a Master of Divinity degree from Pacific Lutheran Theological Seminary in Berkeley, California. He was one of three openly gay seminarians who gained national publicity in 1988 for challenging the Evangelical Lutheran Church in America's policy against ordination of gay men and lesbians.

The Reverend Eric H. F. Law, an Episcopal priest, works as consultant/trainer in multicultural organization development. He is the author of *The Wolf Shall Dwell with the Lamb: A Spirituality for Multicultural Leadership* (Chalice Press, 1993). A composer and performer of church music, he has published three songbooks with accompanying recordings.

The Reverend Dr. Eleanor L. McLaughlin is a church historian and Episcopal priest. She has taught medieval church history, spirituality, women's history, and feminist theory at Wellesley College, Andover-Newton Theological School, and Mount Holyoke College. An accomplished retreat leader and spiritual director, she is an assisting priest at Grace Episcopal Church, Amherst, Massachusetts. She is completing a book, *Uncovering the Body of God: Flesh and Femininity in Western Christian Spirituality*. The mother of two grown daughters, she lives in Southampton, Massachusetts, with her partner Betsy, a clinical psychologist.

Nathan Meckley, M. Mus., studied music at Westminster Choir College in Princeton, New Jersey, and the University of Southern California in Los Angeles. An instructor in the sexuality studies department of Samaritan College, he is enrolled in the Master of Divinity program at the School of Theology at Claremont, in California.

The Reverend Stephen J. Moore is the senior pastor of Grace Chapel Metropolitan Community Church in Santa Barbara, California. His pastoral commitment is to create progressive, inclusive spiritual communities where diversity is celebrated. His scholarly interests include biblical studies, reconstructionist feminist theology, and Latin American liberation theology.

Diann L. Neu, feminist liturgist and therapist, is cofounder and codirector of WATER, the Women's Alliance for Theology, Ethics and Ritual, in Silver Spring, Maryland. She holds Master of Divinity and Master of Sacred Theology degrees from the Jesuit School of Theology in Berkeley, California, and a Master's in Social Work from the Catholic University of America in Washington, D.C.

Christine Nusse is a native of France where she joined the Order of the Little Sisters of the Gospel. She left the order after coming out and then became involved with Dignity in New York. In 1982, she cofounded the Conference for Catholic Lesbians, and she currently participates in a base community called Lesbian Catholics Witnessing for Change. She lives with her lover, Pat, in New York.

Sylvia Perez has fulfilled one of her dreams by kayaking in Alaska, and she looks forward to white-water rafting through the Grand Canyon. She lives with her partner, Jane, in Oakland, California. She describes her spirituality as nurtured through the love of her friends and family.

The Reverend Elder Troy Perry is the founder and moderator of the Universal Fellowship of Metropolitan Community Churches. He founded the UFMCC in 1968 after his Pentecostal church defrocked him for being gay. Since UFMCC's founding, he has been a leading activist for lesbian and gay civil rights. In great demand as a speaker in the United States and elsewhere, he maintains a full travel schedule, preaching in a different region almost every weekend. He is the author of *The Lord Is My Shepherd and He Knows I'm Gay* (Nash Publishing Corp., 1972) and *Don't Be Afraid Anymore*

(St. Martin's Press, 1990). Perry resides in Silverlake, California, with his lover of nine years, Phillip Ray DeBlieck.

The Reverend Michael S. Piazza is the senior pastor of Cathedral of Hope Metropolitan Community Church, the world's largest MCC with an active membership of more than 1,200. A native of Georgia, he has bachelor degrees in history and psychology from the Valdosta State College in Georgia, a Master of Divinity from Candler School of Theology at Emory University in Atlanta, and is currently a doctoral candidate at Austin Presbyterian Seminary. From 1973 to 1981, Rev. Piazza pastored United Methodist churches. In 1981, he became associate pastor of an MCC in Atlanta. He pastored St. Luke's MCC in Jacksonville, Florida, from 1983 to 1987, then moved to Dallas to assume his present position.

The Reverend A. Stephen Pieters, B.S., M. Div., is the field director of AIDS ministry for the Universal Fellowship of Metropolitan Community Churches. Diagnosed with AIDS-related complex in 1982 and AIDS/Kaposi's sarcoma and lymphoma in 1984, Rev. Pieters is one of the long-term survivors profiled in Michael Callen's book, *Surviving AIDS*. He has served on the boards of directors of various AIDS-related organizations, including the AIDS National Interfaith Network. He has been profiled in numerous media appearances. Pieters has traveled throughout North America, Australia, and Western Europe to share his journey of living with HIV/AIDS.

The Reverend Zalmon Sherwood, an Episcopal priest, has worked as a church musician, parish priest, and prison chaplain. Author of *Kairos: Confessions of a Gay Priest* (Alyson), he divides his time between northern Michigan and Florida's Gulf Coast.

The Reverend James E. Snight Jr. served in the Archdiocese of Washington, D.C., for more than ten years. He has also been active as a minister for Dignity/USA for ten years. A native of Washington, D.C., Rev. Snight earned a Master of Divinity degree from Catholic University in 1986.

The Reverend Dr. Jane Adams Spahr has been a cause célèbre in the struggle for lesbian/gay ordination and deployment in the Presbyterian Church (U.S.A.). She is associated with the Spectrum Center for Gay/Lesbian/Bisexual Concerns, which is in partnership with the Downtown United Presbyterian Church, Rochester, New York. Through a fund called That All May Freely Serve, she travels as a lesbian evangelist throughout the United States, where she is in great demand as a speaker and preacher. She is the mother of Jim and Chet, and the partner of the Reverend Coni Staff, who is a minister in the Universal Fellowship of Metropolitan Community Churches.

The Reverend Paul A. Tucker is director of pastoral care at the Cathedral of Hope Metropolitan Community Church in Dallas. He holds a bachelor's degree from Birmingham Southern College and a Master of Divinity degree from Candler School of Theology in Atlanta. After serving as a United

Methodist pastor in the North Alabama Conference for two years, Rev. Tucker has served as a UFMCC pastor for eighteen years in Birmingham, Alabama; Asheville, North Carolina; Nashville, Tennessee; and Dallas.

The Reverend Carol A. West is associate pastor of Cathedral of Hope Metropolitan Community Church, Dallas. With a bachelor's degree in English from the University of North Texas and a Master of Liberal Arts from Texas Christian University, she spent seventeen years as a high school English teacher. She has held UFMCC clergy credentials since 1990.

The Reverend Elder Nancy Wilson has served on the Board of Elders of the Universal Fellowship of Metropolitan Community Churches since 1976, and she became vice moderator of the denomination in 1993. Chief Ecumenical Officer for more than a decade, she is also responsible for UFMCC's relations with the World Council of Churches and countless national, regional, and local church councils. A native of Plainview, New York, she received a Master of Divinity from Saints Cyril and Methodius Seminary (Roman Catholic) in Orchard Lake, Michigan. Reverend Wilson has been senior pastor of Metropolitan Community Church of Los Angeles since 1986. With Malcolm Boyd, she coedited *Amazing Grace: Stories of Lesbian and Gay Faith* (Crossing Press, 1991).

National Lesbian/Gay Christian Organizations

Affirmation/Mormons
Box 46022, Los Angeles, CA 90046; (213) 255–7251

Affirmation/United Methodists
Box 1021, Evanston, IL 60204; (708) 475–0499

American Baptists Concerned
872 Erie St., Oakland, CA 94610; (510) 465–8652

Axios: Eastern and Orthodox Christian Gay Men and Women
P.O. Box 990, Village Station, New York, NY 10014

Brethren/Mennonite Council for Lesbian and Gay Concerns
Box 65724, Washington, DC 20035; (202) 462–2595

CLOUT (Christian Lesbians OUT Together)
P.O. Box 460808, San Francisco, CA 94114

Conference for Catholic Lesbians
Box 436, Planetarium Station, New York, NY 10024; (718) 921–0463

Dignity/USA (Roman Catholic)
1500 Massachusetts Ave., N.W., Suite 11, Washington, DC 20005; (202) 861–0017

Emergence International (Christian Scientist)
Box 9161, San Rafael, CA 94912; (415) 485–1881

Evangelicals Concerned
311 E. 72nd St., Suite 1-G, New York, NY 10021; (212) 517–3171

Friends for Lesbian/Gay Concerns (Quaker)
Box 222, Sumneytown, PA 18084; (215) 234–8424

Gay, Lesbian, and Affirming Disciples Alliance (Disciples of Christ)
P.O. Box 19223, Indianapolis, IN 46219; (319) 324–6231

Integrity, Inc. (Episcopal)
Box 19561, Washington, DC 20036; (201) 868–2485

Lutherans Concerned
Box 10461, Ft. Dearborn Station, Chicago, IL 60610

National Gay Pentecostal Alliance
Box 1391, Schenectady, NY 12301; (518) 372–6001

Presbyterians for Lesbian/Gay Concerns
Box 38, New Brunswick, NJ 08903; (908) 249–1016

Reformed Church in America Gay Caucus
Box 8174, Philadelphia, PA 19101

Seventh Day Adventist Kinship International
P.O. Box 7320, Laguna Niguel, CA 92677; (213) 876–2076

United Church Coalition for Lesbian/Gay Concerns (United Church of
Christ)
18 N. College St., Athens, OH 45701; (614) 593–7301

Unity Fellowship
5149 W. Jefferson Blvd., Los Angeles, CA 90016; (213) 936–4949

Universal Fellowship of Metropolitan Community Churches
5300 Santa Monica Blvd. # 304, Los Angeles, CA 90029; (213) 464–5100

Selected Bibliography

The following list represents a selection of the many books that address issues of inclusive worship and alternative liturgies:

Anderson, Vienna Cobb. *Prayers of Our Hearts in Word and Action*. New York: Crossroad, 1991.

Ayers, Tess, and Paul Brown. *The Essential Guide to Lesbian and Gay Weddings*. HarperSanFrancisco, 1993.

Butler, Becky, ed. *Ceremonies of the Heart: Celebrating Lesbian Unions*. Seattle: The Seal Press, 1990.

Driver, Tom F. *The Magic of Ritual: Our Need for Liberating Rites That Transform Our Lives and Our Communities*. San Francisco: Harper, 1991.

Duck, Ruth C., and Maren C. Tirabassi, eds. *Touch Holiness: Resources for Worship*. New York: Pilgrim Press, 1990.

Feinstein, David, and Peg Elliott Mayo. *Rituals for Living and Dying*. HarperSanFrancisco, 1990.

Glaser, Chris. *Coming Out to God: Prayers for Lesbians and Gay Men, Their Families and Friends*. Louisville, Ky.: Westminster/John Knox Press, 1991.

———. *The Word Is Out: The Bible Reclaimed for Lesbians and Gay Men*. HarperSanFrancisco, 1994.

Kozak, Pat, and Janet Schaffran. *More Than Words: Prayer and Ritual for Inclusive Communities*. Oak Park, IL: Meyer-Stone, 1988.

Mitchell, Rosemary Catalano, and Gail Anderson Ricciuti. *Birthings and Blessings: Liberating Worship Services for the Inclusive Church*. New York: Crossroad, 1992.

———. *Birthings and Blessings II: More Liberating Worship Services for the Inclusive Church*. New York: Crossroad, 1993.

Morley, Janet. *All Desires Known*. Wilton, CT: Morehouse-Barlow, 1988.

Neu, Diann L. *Women Church Celebrations*. Silver Spring, MD: WATER (Women's Alliance for Theology, Ethics and Ritual), 1985.

Stuart, Elizabeth, ed. *Daring to Speak Love's Name: A Gay and Lesbian Prayer Book*. London: Hamish Hamilton, 1992.